from the fold | TO THE FLOCK

Entering the Freedom of True Church Life

Neil Silverberg

FROM THE FOLD TO THE FLOCK

MASTER PRESS

A Master Press Cover Design
Cover Photo by Troy Krombholz (watchlightministries.com)
Back Cover Photo by Peter Zvonar/Shutterstock.com

Printed in the United States

FROM THE FOLD TO THE FLOCK
ISBN 978-0-9913121-0-8

For information:

MASTER PRESS
3405 ISLAND BAY WAY, KNOXVILLE, TN 37931

Mail to: publishing@ masterpressbooks.com

Contents

Foreword.. 4

Introduction... 7

Chapter One: From the Fold to the Flock............................. 11

Chapter Two: Out of the Fold.................................... 21

Chapter Three: The Modern Folds of Christendom................. 29

Chapter Four: Outside the Fold's Walls.................................... 39

Chapter Five: The Great Shepherd of the Sheep...................... 51

Chapter Six: The Chief Shepherd.. 61

Chapter Seven: The Sheep of His Pasture.............................. 69

Chapter Eight: Life in the Flock.. 81

Foreword

Since the day of my own conversion, I have passionately loved the church of Jesus Christ regardless of her condition. I do not write these things as one who has stood aloof, but as one who totally identifies with other believers in my locality. That is important to understand since I have taken it upon myself to criticize her. I do so as a member, not one who has been soured or is embittered by a bad church experience.

After twenty-five years of immersion in church life, I am more convinced than ever before of the truth of what is written in this book. Amazingly, it has also made me more tolerant of those whose understanding and experience of the church is less than Biblical. In fact, I continue to relate to groups of believers and churches who do not view the church the way it is presented in this work, as well as those who do. I am certain that far too many believers who see these things have cut themselves off from vital relationships with other believers in the church who don't. Sometimes such separation is unavoidable, but often it is not.

With that in mind, I present this brief teaching in the hope they will effectively help two groups of God's people. The first group constitutes the majority and is comprised of those whose own experience of the church has become dull and lifeless and have all but abandoned any hope that it could ever be different. My desire is to excite them to the possibilities of a church experience that is everything they ever hoped it would be. By that, I do not intend to paint a picture of church life that is free from problems or difficulties; indeed, those who venture to go this way are assured of a much more difficult and dangerous life. I also want to encourage all those who have started on the road and feel like they are utterly alone. May these words assure you that you are not alone and there are many fellow-pilgrims who are walking with you.

To the countless thousands of pilgrims throughout the ages who have found the courage to follow their Shepherd fully, I sincerely dedicate these words.

Introduction

This is a book about the church. Thousands have already been written about her so why the need for one more? As you read, I believe you will find this message timely and true. The Lord gave this teaching to me several years ago but it was not time to share it. As the Holy Spirit brought it to my remembrance recently, I recognized it to be a "for such a time as this" teaching opportunity.

This book, while about the church, does not deal with any single, specific aspect of the church such as leadership, evangelism, or some facet of the church's ministry. Rather, it deals mainly with presuppositions—the ones we all have about the church and the way she is "supposed" to function. We aren't to be faulted for having them; indeed, everyone does. To live is to presuppose certain things to be true. When it comes to Christianity though, our presuppositions can be a help or a hindrance. This issue is not whether we should have presuppositions, but whether the ones we have are Biblical rather than borrowed from the culture, religion, or our own limited viewpoint.

Most believers could give a fairly Biblical definition of the church. Yet, that is just the problem. While we know how to define it technically, we have lived so long with a certain paradigm; we cannot envision it looking any way else. That is where this book will be most helpful. It challenges the traditional paradigm and the presuppositions commonly associated with it. Rather than accepting the church as she is and taking up a particular aspect of ministry or church life, this book deals with what I believe is the core issue in any discussion of the church. And it does so by examining a particular segment of the teaching of Jesus the Messiah, the so-called Parable of the Good Shepherd found in the tenth chapter of the Gospel of John.

There is another reason I hope the reader will find this work important. There are few works about the church that begin with this teaching of Jesus as a foundation for understanding the church. Apart from examining Christ's teaching regarding the church given at Caesarea Philippi (Matthew 16:13-19), most works on the church have focused primarily on the book of Acts and Epistles. The general thinking has been that Jesus himself said little about the church and that not until the dawning of the Apostolic Age did it really come into view so naturally that must be our starting point. While it is true that theology regarding the church did not fully develop until the apostles started their ministries, it is incorrect to assume that Jesus spoke little about the church. The truth is, the apostles received their foundational understanding of the church from the teaching of the Son of God during his earthly ministry.

That being said this present work is not an examination of all the relevant texts in the Gospels regarding the church, but focuses on the Parable of the Good Shepherd only. There are many other Gospel texts that could be cited but that is not the purpose of this work. This work examines closely Christ's teaching in that particular portion of John's Gospel and then seeks to apply the principles from that section to the church today.

My original intent was a work much longer in scope than this present volume. But, once engaged in writing, I restrained myself from following where I am naturally inclined to go. The result is a much shorter book which I think is better suited to my original purpose. . . which is to cause the reader to think about particular issues rather than supplying answers to every question raised.

I can't help feeling that most of the church will see little relevance for this work (and others like it) until a later hour. A great revolution is dawning, yet most of the church world is oblivious to it. When Martin Luther first made rumblings about his great discovery of the grace of God few took notice until the whole of Europe was ablaze with his Gospel! In that sense this work is prophetic, speaking of things which presently have little significance, but eventually will capture the attention of the Christian world.

I am not the only voice speaking these things in this present hour. All over the earth a company of brave forerunners are exploring the rich pasture lands of authentic church life and are reporting what they have found. Bolstered by those who have gone before they move on confidently, assured that as the Day approaches they will be justified. To all those Bravehearts and to all who are yet to join their company, I dedicate these words. Maranatha!

CHAPTER ONE

From the Fold to the Flock

Most readers of the fourth Gospel are aware that its writer, John, the son of Zebedee, composed his account around seven unique miracles which Jesus performed. John tells us that Jesus performed many more works than these — so many in fact that all the books in the world could not contain them (John 20:25), yet these seven were specially selected by John for a predetermined purpose. It is not that they were the most stupendous works that Jesus did for they certainly were not. Rather, John selected these seven miracles in order that through them his readers might be brought to a saving faith in Jesus of Nazareth as the Messiah, the Son of God (20:31).

While the Synoptics (Matthew, Mark, Luke) refer to Jesus' deeds as "miracles" or "works of power", John simply calls them signs. In John's Gospel this term has great significance. In the Synoptics, a miracle refers to the fact that the work lies in the realm of the supernatural and occurs through the suspension of natural laws. A "sign", on the other hand, refers primarily to the spiritual nature of the miracle and not merely its supernatural origin (though that is inferred). John therefore, selected these seven notable deeds not merely to demonstrate that Jesus was able to suspend natural laws, but to reveal the true essence of the person of Jesus of Nazareth. In this regard, they are not unlike signs on a highway directing a motorist to a certain destination. The purpose of the sign is not to draw attention to itself, but to point away to the traveler's ultimate destination and inform him of how near or far ahead it is. In the same way, John's signs are like clearly marked road signs, pointing away from the work itself and revealing the real essence of the One who performed them.

> John's signs are like road signs, **pointing away** from the *WORK* itself and *revealing* the **real essence** of the **One** who performed them.

A good example of how Jesus' miracles were signs can be found in the sixth chapter of John's Gospel and the account of the miracle of the multiplication of the loaves and fishes. While the miracle itself was an extraordinary work of power only God could perform, its real meaning lies in what it revealed about Jesus himself (John 6:59). Following the miracle, John records Jesus' words to those who had witnessed the miracle in the synagogue at Capernaum. It is there that he reveals himself to them as the "true bread of heaven", the One who alone sustains life (6:32-35). Thus the miracle of the

multiplying of the loaves and the fishes while an actual work of extraordinary power in the physical realm was a sign to them. *It pointed them to Jesus as the true Bread for their souls*, something which many of them were not ready to receive and subsequently left him (6:66). So while the miracle provided men with food and sustained them physically, its true meaning culminates in what it revealed about the Messiah and ultimately their relationship to him. In this way we are able to see these seven deeds as unique windows which allow us to view the inner life of Jesus Christ and thus gain a deeper understanding of the meaning of his person.

The Sign of the Healing of the Man Born Blind

One of the greatest signs performed by Jesus in the Gospel of John is the healing of the man born blind from birth (John 9:1-2). Occasioned by a question from the disciples as to the reason for his blindness, the Lord refused to accommodate their speculations and promptly applied mud to the man's eyes sending him to wash in the Pool of Siloam (9:3-7). The man did and immediately regained his sight.

The healing of this man born blind caused quite a stir in Jerusalem since he had formerly been a prominent beggar in the city. Some tried to deny that it was the same man they had previously seen begging at the temple, but his neighbors insisted that he was the same man. The man himself assured them that he was the one they had previously known and told them how by obeying the word of Jesus he had now received his sight. Amazed at the obvious miracle yet unsure as to what to do, they determined it best to send him to the Pharisees the religious leaders of the day who had already determined that if anyone should confess Jesus as the Messiah he would be put out of the synagogue (9:22).

From The Fold to the Flock

These, therefore were not unbiased men willing to listen carefully to objective testimony about Jesus, but men who were doing all in their power to squelch the movement growing up around Jesus of Nazareth. They had been unable to do so until now and the presence of a man blind from birth who was healed certainly did not help matters. They must now find a way to discredit not only Jesus himself, but the formerly blind beggar as well.

Perhaps we have had occasion for ourselves to witness the interrogation by religious leaders of one who has been specially touched by God. Many times when God is at work in the midst of religious systems rigidly controlled by those with a vested interest in protecting their own positions there is the attempt to discredit those who claim a fresh experience with God. Threatened with the loss of prestige or position men will lie, manipulate, or do anything else in order to maintain control. In such an atmosphere truthfulness and honesty is the last thing allowed to stand. Men may speak and act as though they were impartial, yet the real issue is their need to save their own reputation.

That is what makes the account of the formerly blind beggar's testimony so wonderful. Into the midst of these men with their personal agendas comes this one with no motive other than that of relating the truth of what he had seen and what he had personally experienced. How refreshing such openness and honesty is in the midst of such duplicity! Yet it is a direct threat to the powers that be and must be discredited. To do otherwise may be doing something outside of their authority and without their approval and this they could never accept. Rather, they question him under the guise of desiring the truth, yet all along their real motive is to find some way to discredit what he was saying. To them this was far better than having to deal with the implication of an evident miracle that had

14

occurred in their midst.

After questioning him and being unable to find anything wrong with his story they attempted to disprove his claim to have been born blind. his parents were brought in and interrogated, but they only substantiated that he was indeed their son and that his eyes were now opened. Again, the man was brought back in and asked to repeat his account of what had happened. Aware of their duplicity the formerly blind beggar was becoming exasperated. He had already told them – did they want to hear again so that they could become his disciples? This was more than they could take and the Pharisees jointly reviled the man. They were the disciples of no one but Moses and could confidently say where Moses came from – as for this man they had no idea where He had come from.

At this the man who was healed issued a response cutting to the heart of their religious pretense. How could they claim to have no idea where this man came from when he had just opened the eyes of a man born blind from birth? Surely such signs substantiated his claims. If He were not from God, He could do nothing (John 9:33). Such truth uttered by one who was a witness to its reality was more for them than they could bear. They would not be lectured by one born in sin (a common Jewish teaching as to why men were born blind) and rose up, casting him

> While those who
> **NEVER** SAW LIGHT *(blind)*
> were *now receiving*
> *their sight physically,*
> those who **COULD SEE** PHYSICALLY
> **WERE BLINDED** to the
> **REAL Person** who now
> stood in their midst.

out of the synagogue. In the space of just a few hours this man had now gone from living in total darkness to receiving his sight and as a result he was excommunicated from the community of faith... all because of his willingness to testify to the truth regarding Jesus and the opening of his eyes.

The Reason for the Parable

That is John's account recorded in the ninth chapter of his Gospel of the opening of the eyes of the man blind from birth. Yet like the other signs recorded by John this one is also followed by an in-depth discourse in which Jesus reveals the real meaning of the sign. The miracle was that Jesus of Nazareth had opened the eyes of a man born blind, yet its real meaning lies in the revelation it sets forth regarding the Son of God.

To understand the meaning of the sign, it is first necessary to follow the story of the blind man after he was cast out of the synagogue. The text says Jesus himself upon hearing of the formerly blind beggar's excommunication found the man and came to him (John 9:35). This is only one of two passages in all four Gospels in which it is said that Jesus himself *found* someone. Certainly this displays the majestic love of the Son of God for this man that He came to his aid at the very moment of excommunication. Yet, it was not only love for this man that drove the Lord to seek him out. He was also desirous of revealing the true meaning of the sign which he had performed. "For judgment I have come into this world, so that the blind will see and those who see will become blind" (9:39). The very purpose of his coming into this world was for judgment here defined as the opening of the eyes of those who were blind and blinding the eyes of those who could see. The intended meaning was obvious. While those who never saw light (blind) were now receiving their sight physically, those who could see physically were blinded to the real Person who now stood in their midst. It is not that the Lord intentionally caused the blindness; it was simply an inevitable by-product of his coming.

The teaching which concludes the ninth chapter of John continues in chapter ten. Jesus immediately began to speak a parable commonly known as the "Parable of the Good Shepherd". Most readers of Scripture have known and loved this parable for its beauty and the powerful imagery it conveys. Unfortunately, many readers have assumed that since this parable begins a new chapter it has no relationship with that which preceded it; namely, the story of the healing of the man born blind and his subsequent excommunication from Israel. It is not difficult to understand how one would conclude this. For one thing, many Bible readers often assume that a new chapter in itself signifies new subject matter and that is often not the case. We should remember that the chapter and verse headings found in our English Bibles are not divinely inspired, but were supplied by the translators so that we can more easily move through Scripture. This is a convenience for which we ought to be thankful, but like so many conveniences it is one for which we pay dearly. To study the Scripture properly therefore we must ignore these artificial divisions and follow the Biblical author's train of thought. It is context that matters which means that we must ignore chapter and verse headings if we want to discover the meaning of a passage of Scripture.

Why have I taken the time to explain this important aspect of Biblical exegesis? Because it has special significance in regards to understanding our Lord's teaching in the Parable of the Good Shepherd. If we conclude that the parable contains a new body of teaching which has no relationship with that which preceded it (the account of the healing of the blind man) then we may miss its meaning entirely. While admiring its beauty and its cogent statements about Jesus, its real significance may be lost. That is because our Lord's words in the parable uttered in the presence of the man that had been cast out as well as the Pharisees was vitally connected to the story of the blind man's healing and subsequent rejection by the leaders of Israel.

> The *Parable of the Good Shepherd* describes the nature of the KINGDOM which **Christ** came to establish.

At first glance, they may not seem to be related at all. There is no doubt that the parable is beautiful and contains some of the most salient declarations about himself that Jesus ever made. Yet the question we should ask is, "Why did Jesus choose this moment to compare himself to an ancient shepherd who cares for all of the needs of his sheep?" What seeming relationship was there between his words and the excommunication of the formerly blind beggar? Besides, would it not have been more profitable in the presence of the Pharisees in whose hearing our Lord spoke to have uttered a parable more fitting to the moment like the Parable of the Landowner or that of the Wicked Tenants? It would seem so, but that is not what our Lord does. Like so much of his teachings, at first glance these words don't seem to fit the moment. Yet, as we shall see upon closer examination, these words were perfectly fitted to that moment in a way that is quite disarming.

The simplest starting point in understanding this parable and our Lord's purpose in uttering it is that it provided a reason for our Lord's reception of the man whom the Pharisees had cast out. We must remember the chain of events that led to the uttering of these words. After Jesus had healed the blind man, he left the area so that no one knew where he was. This was followed by the interrogation of the man by the Pharisees and his eventual excommunication. Immediately (or soon afterwards), upon hearing of his being cast out, Jesus heard about it and came to him. Then, in the presence of both the man and the Pharisees Jesus uttered those clarion words intended especially for the Pharisees. They were those who claimed that they could see but who by Jesus' coming were actually being made blind while those who were physically blind were now having their eyes opened both physically and spiritually. As we have already seen, that teaching was intended to illuminate the real meaning of the sign which Jesus performed. It was then, with the Pharisees still present, that Jesus uttered the parable which fills entirely the tenth chapter of the Gospel of John.

Still the question remains, "What relationship does the parable have to these events?" It is not until carefully examining the parable itself that we will begin to find an answer. For now it will suffice to make only a general statement regarding its purpose (we will deal with it more thoroughly in the next chapter). *In simplest terms, the Parable of the Good Shepherd was directed at helping to describe the nature of the kingdom which Christ came to establish.* It was uniquely aimed at illuminating the difference between that which was the typical experience of the sheep in Judaism and that which the sheep would enjoy under the leadership of the Good Shepherd who would "lay down his life for the sheep." We will take this up more thoroughly in the next chapter.

CHAPTER 2

Out of the Fold

The story which Jesus told in the Parable of the Good Shepherd was based on a familiar occurrence in Israel; that of an ancient shepherd caring for his sheep. Every Israelite in Jesus' day knew what a shepherd did and what was involved in caring for his sheep. We, who are from the West, far from the agrarian society of the ancient Middle East need an explanation of these things. Without it we will find it difficult to understand the parable and its teaching since it is based on both the actions of a shepherd in caring for his sheep, and the movements of the flock while it roams about the countryside seeking pasture lands to feed upon.

One of the first things we must understand is that the action of the story begins in a fold, a simple enclosure to which sheep were brought at night to afford them temporary protection from wolves and other dangers. The walls were often made of stones piled together upon which briar thorns were placed, thus making it difficult to scale. There was never a roof in a fold so that it was always open to the evening sky. The only entrance into the fold was a door which was really not a door, but an opening in the wall where the sheep entered and departed. Normally, the shepherd would lie down in the doorway at night. This meant literally that the only way into the fold was "by him."

Typically, more than one flock would enter a fold at night. In the morning after the various flocks had rested securely each shepherd would awaken and call "his own sheep by name" and they would leave the fold and follow the shepherd. The sheep knew the unique voice of their shepherd and would not dare to follow another. This is obviously what Jesus meant when He said that the sheep "do not recognize a stranger's voice" (John 10:5). They are thus trained in hearing only the voice of the shepherd. The shepherd would lead the sheep out of the fold to begin their day following him into the rich pasture lands upon which they would feed to their heart's content.

Once the sheep left the fold, there were many dangers. Inside the walls of the fold they were safe, but once outside their only security lie in carefully listening to the voice of the shepherd. If they do not listen carefully to his voice and wander from the flock they may be devoured by wolves which lie in wait. Listening carefully to the voice of the shepherd therefore is not a luxury – it is a necessity for sheep once they have left the fold!

Once out of the fold sheep are always referred to as a *flock*. We must make a distinction in reading the parable between the *fold* and the *flock*. The fold is important, yet it is simply a temporary holding pen for the sheep. Their real desire is not to spend their time penned up and confined in the fold but in the *flock,* freely roaming with the shepherd on the open fields in search of the richest pasture lands. In the great Shepherd-Psalm (Psalm 23), David beautifully describes an entire day in the life of the sheep from the moment they first awake and behold the shepherd's form to their final moments before falling asleep under his watchful care. The Psalm equally describes the dangers that the sheep face during their time outside the fold. Nevertheless in this beautiful Psalm, David carefully portrays the main pursuit of sheep in a flock — not confined in the fold, but roaming freely in green pastures eating to their heart's content.

The Meaning of the Parable

That is the story which Jesus told in the presence of the Pharisees after receiving the man who had been born blind whom He had healed. Obviously, the elements of the story are not difficult to understand. Yet this still does not explain why Jesus told this parable at this particular time. What did he intend by this beautiful story of a shepherd and his relationship with his sheep?

> As the sheep *hear* THE CALL they **must** **LEAVE** the fold.

We have already seen that the action in the parable begins with a shepherd entering a fold and calling out his own sheep by name: "I tell you the truth, the man who does not enter the sheep pen (fold) by the gate, but climbs in by some other way, is a thief and a robber. The man who enters by the gate is the shepherd of his sheep" (John 10:1-2). In relation to the events of the preceding chapter the meaning of the parable begins to come clear. The Pharisees had just cast the man born blind out of the synagogue. When Jesus

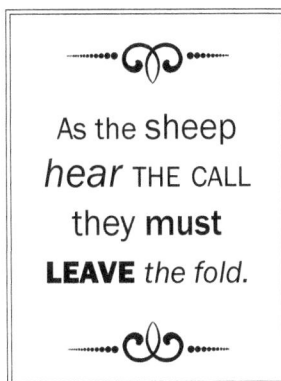

> The old **forms**
> of Judaism
> could **not contain**
> the *life*
> Jesus was giving
> to His *people.*

heard about it, he immediately found him and revealed himself to the man as the Messiah (9:35-38). By so doing, he demonstrated this man was one of his sheep and that it was necessary for him to "leave the fold in order to enter the flock." The Lord's intention to portray Israel as the fold in the parable should be quite obvious. More specifically, behind his words *Jesus was revealing that he was now calling the true sheep to leave the fold of Judaism and enter the flock.* The main point of the parable therefore, is as the sheep hear the call they must leave the fold. It would be impossible for the true sheep to remain in the fold and follow the shepherd simultaneously.

That this is the meaning of the parable becomes clearer when comparing it with other teachings given by our Lord during his earthly ministry. At various times and in differing ways, he had announced that he had come to do something utterly new, something incompatible with that which the sheep had known in traditional Judaism. Thus the Lord spoke of putting "new wine in new wineskins." It was impossible that the old forms which characterized Judaism could contain the life that Jesus was giving to his people. In the same way, this parable also demonstrated that what he had come to do could never be contained in the forms of first century Judaism. The true sheep *must* leave the fold and enter the flock.

Yet in his teaching Jesus did not undermine the importance of what had gone before. Even though he was now calling his sheep out of the fold it had been necessary for the sheep to be temporarily sheltered there. The purpose of God began with the Jewish nation and the covenant that God made with the people of Israel. This should help us to understand what Jesus was teaching at this time. He was not calling the sheep to repudiate their heritage as Israelites, members of that distinct community to which God had first revealed himself and brought them into covenant with himself. The fold was not Israel, but what Israel had become; a religion of restriction characterized by rules and restrictions. These things (not being part of Israel) were not compatible with life in the new kingdom. The new kingdom was characterized by the freedom which sheep in a flock experience – moving in and out on the open mountains, grazing on the richest pasture lands (John 10:9). How can life in the cramped fold compare to the freedom of following the shepherd on the open fields?

The analogy of first century Judaism to a fold is very revealing. For one thing, sheep within a fold are very restricted since it allows little movement (something we will deal more fully with later). Anyone familiar with Judaism's strictures is aware of how it cramped the life of the ordinary Israelite. The rabbis spoke of the "hedge of the Law" protecting Israel from Gentile defilement but that hedge, while seeking to protect, actually constricted the life. Each day was governed by hundreds of rules and regulations which every Israelite was expected to meticulously observe (Judaism had reduced the Law to a mere 633 commandments!) The intention may have been to protect the common Israelite, but the result was an intolerable weight by the demands of a Law he could not keep. The apostle Paul says as much when he refers to the Law in the Galatian epistle as a "yoke of slavery" (Galatians 5:1).

Other Sheep

Jesus was now calling the sheep to leave the fold and enter the flock. The flock was meant to characterize the new life the sheep would enjoy under the New Covenant. No longer was it a matter of keeping rules and regulations, but of carefully listening to the voice of the Shepherd. Following the Shepherd meant that the sheep would "have life, and have it to the full" (10:10). This is true life indeed which could not be restricted by the old forms of Judaism. Not until the Shepherd *"laid down his life for the sheep"* and was glorified would it be fully entered into, but once that occurred, life in the flock would be open to all the sheep (10:15).

> The **CHURCH** is **ONE** *flock*... **ONE** *people* of **God** **JOINED TOGETHER** by the **FINISHED WORK** of the **TRUE** *Shepherd.*

In the parable Jesus spoke of bringing *"other sheep"* into the flock (10:16). This is a clear reference to his intention to gather sheep that were not of the fold (Gentiles), and include them in the Messianic kingdom. Together with those of the fold of Israel there would be "one flock and one shepherd." In this way the parable has a direct reference to the "church age"; that time after the Shepherd had "laid down his life" and returned to his glory, pouring out his life-giving Spirit on the church. It was at that time that there would be a manifestation in the church of what the apostle Paul termed "one new man"; Jew and Gentile united in Christ in one body

(Ephesians 2:15). The church was one flock; neither a Jewish flock nor a Gentile flock, but one people of God joined together by the finished work of the true Shepherd.

Of course Jesus' word that he would bring "other sheep that are not of this sheep pen" would be the basis for one of the most difficult issues the early church would have to face. The inclusion of the Gentiles into the Messianic kingdom not as second-class citizens, but as full members of the covenant community (Ephesians 2:19) would not gain full acceptance easily. Those still in the fold were accustomed to the security which the walls of the fold afforded them. They were not willing to see that protection which the Law provided eroded. This was true not only of those of the stock of Israel who rejected Jesus as Messiah, but also of those Jews who had believed upon him, yet still insisted that the Gentiles should be made to keep the Law as well (Acts 15:1). It was this issue that almost tore apart the Jerusalem church and to which the apostle Paul would devote all of his apostolic energies to refute. While the church in Jerusalem eventually acknowledged that it was grace alone that saved both Jew and Gentile (15:22-29), the battle would rage for many years and serve as a constant thorn in Paul's side.

Applying the Parable to the Church

In the parable we have seen what Jesus intended to convey. He had now come to build his church and it could not be contained within the fold of first Century Judaism. The sheep's identity was now to be found in their relationship to the Shepherd alone. This passage therefore is teaching the church would be comprised of those who would leave the fold of Judaism and, along with all those "other sheep" from among the Gentiles, follow the Shepherd who was calling them to himself.

So far that much is plain. That gives us an accurate interpretation of the parable and its immediate application to Jesus' own day. Yet on the basis of this interpretation we may now also make an application beyond the immediate historical situation. That is, once we are assured we have interpreted the passage properly, we must now look for ways in which to apply to our own situation. Here we shall find the passage applies in a way we might not readily want to admit.

First, it will be helpful to remember that in making application of Scripture to ourselves there are certain principles that we should always keep in mind. One of them is that in order to apply a text properly we must look for comparisons between the Biblical situation and our own. How closely does the story or history related in the Biblical text mirror that of our own? An example of that using our present text might be to make a comparison between ourselves and the Pharisees to whom the parable was spoken. Are there similarities between the way Pharisees thought and we think today? Without a doubt there most definitely are.

This principle of making comparisons is helpful in applying this text to ourselves in at least another significant way. By comparing the folds used to house sheep in the first century to modern church life we shall discover, if honest, many similarities. Of course in saying that, we are drawing a comparison between modern church life and that of first century Judaism typified by the metaphor of the fold. In order to substantiate this statement we must look more closely at the nature of folds and in particular the experience of sheep while in a fold. By doing so, we will be able to understand its application to the modern church as well as the inverse —what life in the flock was intended to be (the subject of later chapters).

CHAPTER THREE

The Modern Folds
of Christendom

When Jesus spoke of himself as the Good Shepherd who was entering the fold to bring out his sheep He was describing the church that he was in the process of building (Matthew 16:16). Although it was necessary for the sheep to have remained in the fold for a time, they were now being called out to enter the flock. The flock would now exist entirely apart from the fold. Now their sole identity was to be found in their relationship to the Shepherd rather than within the four walls of the fold to which they had been accustomed.

This should help us clear up the question as to why, if the church was so important to God, Jesus did not speak about it more clearly during his earthly ministry. The truth is, He did speak about it often, though he only used the actual word "church" twice (Matthew 16:16, 18:15). As we have seen in the Parable of the Good Shepherd, Jesus employed various metaphors to describe it rather than speaking about it directly. The metaphor in the parable before us provides us with a clear understanding of how Jesus himself viewed the church. We have already seen that he saw the church as that which has its origins with the fold of Judaism, yet would eventually exist entirely apart from that.

The Fold and Church Life

In the previous chapter, we began to see that the parable not only sets forth an important historical truth but also has a practical application as well. Modern Christianity, and in particular the way in which most modern churches function are similar to those folds used by ancient shepherds to keep the sheep at night. That is a radical statement and in the remainder of this book I intend to support it fully, but for now it is necessary to simply set it forth.

To understand, we must look more closely at the nature of folds and in particular the experience of sheep while they are in a fold. By so doing, we will be able to understand its application to the modern church as well as the inverse – what life in the flock was intended to be (the subject of later chapters).

Life in the Fold Was Restrictive

The primary reason sheep are brought into a fold at night is for protection. The fold was designed as a temporary holding pen for sheep to rest securely from the threat of wild animals which would attack at night. The fold's walls insured that no animal could enter the fold nor any sheep wander out. The door was the only way into the fold and anyone attempting to enter would have to step over the sleeping shepherd who lie at the entrance way.

While the fold certainly afforded them protection it was by its very nature *restrictive*. Sheep in the fold are not able to roam freely with the shepherd in search of rich pasture lands in which to feed. They were not meant to live their lives penned up. A sheep's life consists of eating and that means that it must be free to roam. Even a cursory reading of David's great Shepherd-Psalm demonstrates that fact. The action begins with the waking moments when the sheep are led out of the fold to begin their day following the shepherd into the open fields. This is the life to which the sheep are called – outside of the fold richly feeding on luxurious pasture lands! It is only at the end of the day that they are brought back to the fold remaining safely within its walls until the start of the next day.

The picture of sheep in a fold is a fitting metaphor for the experience of many of God's people in the church today. Like sheep in a fold they are often severely cramped by a church environment which makes movement near impossible. In recent years numerous books have been published all identifying the culprit — traditional church structures that inhibit rather than release God's sheep. Unfortunately,

> Without **e x e r c i s e,** **God's sheep** are consigned to a life of **p e r p e t u a l** IMMATURITY.

many of them deal only superficially with the real issue; the continued belief that church life occurs within the four walls of church buildings. As long as we continue to think of the church as a place where we go to perform spiritual service we continue to perpetuate a fold—like concept of the church. Yet despite the clear teaching of God's word many churches are so wedded to buildings and programs they could never perceive church life without them. While giving lip service to the clear Biblical truth that the church is not a building, judging from the amount of money and time spent adorning these structures the real values are evident. As a friend of mine once remarked, "Churches are building their own kingdoms and those who aren't have ordered the cement!"

> The traditional
> # VIEW
> of the CHURCH
> as a **PLACE** *where*
> a large number of
> **PASSIVE SHEEP**
> *lie down and wait*
> for the **SHEPHERD**
> to **FEED** them
> **MIRRORS**
> that of the **fold**
> rather than
> the **FLOCK.**

The issue of course is not merely that of buildings (although that is not without significance in God's word), but the proper atmosphere for the development of God's people. As in the growth of any living thing the environment in which something is placed has much to do with its growth. A plant needs good soil if it is to grow but equally important is the climate or environment in which it grows. Even plants growing in the best of soil will not survive in arid or dry climates. So it is that our spiritual environment (church life) has much to do with our spiritual development. *And God has ordained real church life as presented in the New Testament to serve as the only proper climate for the spiritual growth of his people.*

What is needed is a spiritual environment characterized by that of the flock rather than the fold. This has several implications but we will briefly mention two both pertaining to the single word exercise. When we speak of life in the fold being restrictive we mean that the sheep are not free to move about and exercise their true nature as sheep. Therefore spiritual growth is stifled for it is an inevitable law of the kingdom that it is only by exercise that growth can occur (Hebrews 5:12-14). Without exercise, God's sheep are consigned to a life of perpetual immaturity.

How are we to exercise? The first way is in learning to feed upon the rich pastures of God's word for ourselves. Nothing is more debilitating to real spiritual development than the habit of many saints of receiving all their spiritual nourishment from others. While Scripture certainly makes room for those new in Christ to receive the milk of the word from more advanced believers, such a continued dependence on others was never meant to be a way of life. Even the teaching of God's word, while a necessary part of church life (Acts 2:42) was never intended to become a substitute for living by "every word that comes from the mouth of God" (Matthew 4:4). Like Israel of old, God's people are required to gather the manna for themselves. Teaching from those gifted is a blessing for any church, but it can quickly become like manna rotten if we don't learn to gather for ourselves.

The answer is not to banish the teaching of God's word from church life or downplay the role of Scripture in our lives (as some have erroneously concluded). It is to lead the sheep into the green pastures where they learn how to feed for themselves on the rich bounty of God's truth. The traditional view of the church as a place where a large number of passive sheep lie down and wait for the shepherd to feed them mirrors that of the fold rather than the flock. While shepherds and teachers provide an immeasurable wealth for the church of God this must never be viewed as an end in itself, but merely as a provision to supplement what we ourselves receive. Shepherds lead their flocks to the finest fields; once there it is the sheep's responsibility to feed upon it until they are full.

Life in the Fold Was Constrained

Besides receiving spiritual nourishment for themselves, God's people must also exercise themselves through spiritual service using the gifts and abilities that each has been given (I Peter 4:10). It is an invaluable law of the kingdom of God that "only by use comes increase." Therefore, it is in *doing* that believers are built up and established in the faith. As Jesus himself said, "My food is to do the will of him who sent me and to finish his work" (John 4:34).

Yet this is exactly where traditional church life has failed. For the most part, it does not provide room for the ordinary believer to exercise his or her gifts for the edification of the entire body. If life in the fold is severely restricted (the sheep are confined to the four walls), it is also severely *constrained* (the sheep are cramped making movement difficult). Remember, more than one flock would usually share a fold at night and this meant the maximum number of sheep in the smallest amount of space! Such cramped quarters would cause the sheep to constantly butt up against one another; a far cry from the freedom they have when roaming the rich pasture lands under the shepherd's care.

In this regard many churches today, like folds, have become little more than large pens allowing for little spiritual movement. While the sheep are encouraged to be involved in certain activities (coming to church, voting, paying tithes, etc.), they are hindered from participating in the real work of the ministry which God has ordained for all the saints to do (Ephesians 4:12). Ministry in such churches is usually viewed as the sacred possession of a chosen few, rather than the privilege of all. Is it any wonder that the saints remain spiritually immature when they are always kept in the pen? They were not meant to lie in the fold all day eating food provided for them but to roam freely in green pastures.

Often sheep in the fold will imitate other sheep. This may help us to understand another aspect of many churches — *they tend to mistake outward conformity for real change which only comes through inward development.* It is relatively easy to assume that because people are coming to the meetings, singing the songs, paying their tithes, and are involved in the various programs of the church leaders that they are really developing spiritually. Yet often such growth is really only conformity to an environment and learned behavior. Sheep have the unique propensity to simply imitate the behavior of the group members under the guise that they are learning spiritual things.

True spiritual things can only be learned in an environment of real church life (flock) where all man-made restrictions are removed and where God's people can have genuine spiritual experience. One of the most significant ways that characterizes the difference between the flock and the fold is in the way in which church meetings are conducted. In the fold, for the most part, the majority of saints never participate in church meetings. Instead, church leaders lead them through the various stations of worship and ministry. Yet the sheep never dare initiate these things. It is interesting that the New Testament never describes church meetings as "worship services" nor does it insist that such meetings be led exclusively by church leaders. Does that mean that there is not a place for a community of believers to worship together and gather around the teaching of God's word? There most certainly is. *Yet it is important to note that in the only portion of the New Testament where church meetings are thoroughly described (I Corinthians 11-14) their real purpose is not for worship services or listening to sermons, but for eating of the Lord's Supper and for the edification of church members through the exercise of spiritual gifts that each has received (Romans 12:3-8, I Corinthians 12:4-11, I Peter 4:10).*

It should be apparent why such an atmosphere is best suited for spiritual development. People only grow through direct involvement in the things of God. If for the whole of their lives believers remain only on the receiving end they most certainly will remain stunted in their growth. Yet that is exactly the case for most saints in the typical church. They have been raised in an environment in which they have been taught to sit passively as spectators rather than as participators. If they do get involved it is almost invariably in things that are not considered to be real ministry such as sitting on committees, cutting the church lawn, and greeting people. The New Testament speaks of the saints' direct involvement in the work of God including participation in church meetings. Each one is to use what he has received both in edifying the other members when the church is gathered (I Corinthians 14:26), as well as in building up the community as a whole (I Peter 4:10-11).

The functioning of the members in the gatherings of the

church has implications far beyond church meetings themselves. If the saints are unable to function in meetings of the saints what chance is there that they will function outside the church where the real work of God takes place? It is ludicrous to believe that passive saints who are mere spectators in church life will take the responsibility of doing God's work outside the church if they have never learned to take responsibility inside the church. Thus the participation of members in both church meetings and in the local church in general is an important Biblical issue that cannot be ignored if we are serious about "equipping the saints for works of service" (Ephesians 4:12). As we shall see it has a direct bearing on the saints' ability to perform their most important task; outside the walls of the fold following the Shepherd as He continues to gather other sheep to himself.

CHAPTER FOUR

Outside the Fold's Walls

We have already seen that the primary reason sheep are brought into a fold at night is for protection. Behind the fold's walls the sheep were certainly secure. No animal could enter and ravage the flock unless it was willing of course, to go through the shepherd who slept at the door. This was protection all right but it was protection at a cost. For the fold not only protected the sheep from without, it also prevented them from roaming freely on the pasture lands with their shepherd.

Sheep were created not to live in the fold, but to feed on the rich pasture lands of tender green grass. Yet ironically this constitutes their greatest danger as well. Outside the fold they must always be on the watch for wolves which would devour the flock. They must also be careful when following the

> ⸻ ❦ ⸻
>
> Many **churches**
>
> have ERECTED
>
> man-made WALLS
>
> which I S O L A T E
>
> b e l i e v e r s
>
> from **VITAL CONTACT**
>
> with the **world.**
>
> ⸻ ❦ ⸻

shepherd on the narrow mountain tracks not to fall over a precipice. Yes, there are many dangers outside the fold. Yet the sheep would rather be free to roam with the shepherd in the flock than remain safely behind the walls of the fold.

Many local assemblies today operated more like folds than they do flocks. What do we mean by that? Under the guise of protecting believers from the world many churches have erected man-made walls which have in fact totally isolated believers from vital contact with the world. While carried out under the umbrella of "separation from the world" it really is a perversion of the Biblical doctrine. The result has been that while the believer remains safely "in the church" he or she has lost the ability to affect the world for the kingdom of God. This alone should be a sufficient reason for leaving the fold and entering the flock.

The Biblical Doctrine of Separation

In order to understand this more fully it is necessary to underscore an important Biblical truth regarding the church's relationship to the world. Indeed, Scripture teaches that believers are "in the world but not of it" and that they must live a life *separated* from the world. In Scripture the church is presented as an alternative society, a "world within the world."

When a person believes the Gospel, they are rescued from the world and joined to the church where they now live the new life with other believers in the community of the redeemed. From the Bible's perspective therefore every human being is part of a particular community. They are either a member of the old community headed up by Adam, or they have joined God's new community created through the redemptive work of His Son, Jesus Christ. That is why the Bible speaks of being saved not so much in terms of deliverance from hell as deliverance from the world. In the words of the apostle Paul to enter the kingdom of God is to be "rescued from the dominion of darkness and brought into the kingdom of the Son he loves" (Colossians 1:13).

> **D o c t r i n e**
>
> HAS SIMPLY BEEN
>
> **NEGLECTED**
>
> by **M A N Y**
>
> *c h u r c h e s .*

It stands to reason therefore that since the believer is no longer part of the world he must live a life of separation from it. Practically, this means not making alliances with unbelievers such as in marriage and other areas (II Corinthians 6:14-7:1). The whole issue with the Corinthian church was that they lived exactly like their pagan neighbors judging things from worldly standards, having lawsuits with one another, and acting immorally. Paul's reasoning is to persuade them (once again) that since they have received the Spirit of God they must live differently from the world. Their judgments as well as lifestyle must now be shaped by the new life which they have in Christ. In a word, the Spirit within them was holy and called them to a life of complete separation from the world.

Paul had much to say about this vital teaching in his letters, especially those written to the Thessalonians. He remands them that the very Spirit whom they have received and who indwells them is holy and instructs them in these matters (I Thessalonians 4:7-8). Paul makes it clear that those who reject this are not rejecting human teaching, but the teaching of God himself whose presence in the believer's heart testifies to this truth (4:8). Thus, the truth of the believer's separation from the world was a vital part of the apostolic corpus. God had redeemed a people essentially to bring them out of the world and to himself. This meant that each believer must know practically what it means to live a life of separation from this present age and its defilement.

While there is no doubt that the apostolic writers of the New Testament were clear about this truth of separation, the church has not always been. Without oversimplifying we can basically cite two reasons for this. We will look only briefly at the first in order to focus more thoroughly upon the second.

The first is that the doctrine has simply been neglected by many churches. Whether due to the fear of loss of members or the risk of losing popularity, many church leaders have taken a "no mention" approach to the believer's call to separation from the world. This, of course does not exonerate individual believers from their responsibility since the doctrine is clearly taught in Scripture. Yet, the unwillingness of leaders to clearly teach this divine truth must be one of the main reasons for its evident loss in the church and the degree of worldliness among believers. Leaders must once again be willing to proclaim this Biblical truth even if it means losing nominal members whose lives are a contradiction to the message. While the result may mean less professing believers it would certainly be a spiritual boon for the church.

Church leaders have not always been silent regarding this vital New Testament teaching. Until the last few decades many churches regularly emphasized it and expected their members to live accordingly. Of course some churches while recognizing its importance became legalistic in their application of this truth. Under the guise of separation from the world they unwisely characterized every form of enjoyment as worldly and to be shunned. Separation from the world became associated with long faces, blandness, and Elizabethan naiveté. Perhaps that is one reason why many churches chose instead to ignore it completely. Associating it with legalism these churches steered clear of it, yet in so doing they unwittingly rejected the clear Biblical teaching that the believer must live his or her life in complete separation from the world.

Not all believers or churches have neglected this vital truth of separation. Some have attempted to be faithful to the Biblical call to live separated lives, yet in so doing have actually substituted the Scriptural teaching with something else. We should always remember that Satan takes two approaches in attempting to foil believers. The first is to tempt them to neglect the Word of God entirely so that they are in ignorance of its promises and demands. Yet when that fails his approach is to distort the word by mixing it with human ideas and traditions. Then those who hold it may think that they are actually obeying it, but it is so mixed with tradition and man-made ideas that it might as well have been ignored— it amounts to the same thing. That is exactly what Satan has done with the Biblical truth of separation so that in actuality it has become *isolation*. Desiring to be separated from the world most believers are in reality totally isolated from it. They have little or no relationship to it practically — they are neither in the world nor of it. Yet Scripture never calls us to live our lives in complete isolation from unbelievers. Rather, it is to be separated unto God while remaining vitally connected to those who are estranged from him.

The apostle Paul's letters to the church at Corinth confirm this vital difference between separation and isolation. In a previous letter (which has been lost) Paul told them to avoid all contact with immoral people (I Corinthians 5:9-13). The Corinthians, upon reading this, had difficulty understanding the apostle's instruction. Their city, Corinth had a reputation throughout the Roman Empire for debauchery and sexual immorality. To obey the apostle's teaching literally would mean they would have to move from Corinth. The apostle did not mean that of course and he wrote back to the church to tell them that they had misunderstood what he was teaching (and so have we). He was not instructing them to have no contact with unbelievers, but rather with those who call themselves believers and practice such things. *Far from exhorting them to isolation he was actually calling them to remove themselves from other believers who while claiming to be in Christ, had not yet separated themselves from the world.* This is what the apostle taught and what the New Testament teaches regarding the Biblical doctrine of separation.

> ⸻ ❧ ⸻
>
> # True
> # *holiness is*
> # *Beautiful*
> ## and **ATTRACTS**
> ### **SINNERS** *rather*
> ### *than* **REPELS** *them!*
>
> ⸻ ❧ ⸻

Then what should the relationship of the church be towards unbelievers? Since we are called to follow him in this world we may learn much from the way that Jesus lived during his earthly ministry. Did He live in complete isolation from sinners? The calling of Matthew the tax collector provides the clearest example of our Lord's attitude toward sinners. Our Lord not only willingly received him into his kingdom; he also attended a dinner at his house where several known sinners were present (Mark 2:14-15). When the Jewish teachers of the Law, who viewed all association with known sinners as a lack of seriousness in religious matters criticized him, Jesus did not mind at all (2:15). He had come to call sinners to himself and that meant that He must spend time with them in the same way that a physician spends time with his patients (2:17).

We must be clear though that while Jesus did not live his life in isolation from sinners, he nevertheless remained separated from them (Hebrews 7:26). While he was with them he never partook of their sins. He was not there to enjoy their sin but rather to reveal the love of the Father. This meant that he must remain separated from sin while at the same time in vital touch with humanity. The same is true in our own ministry to the world. The presence of the Spirit in our hearts creates an inward barrier between us and the world, yet all the while allowing for free movement among its citizens. This is the practical outworking of the Biblical concept of holiness.

When Jesus sat at Matthew's house he was not attracted to their sin, yet sinners were certainly attracted to him. True holiness is beautiful and attracts sinners rather than repels them (Psalm 29:2). It is not unlike the burning bush which Moses saw in the wilderness (Exodus 3:1-3). At first the sight of a bush burning and not being consumed attracted Moses and bid him to come near. Yet as he approached God could be heard forbidding him to

From The Fold to the Flock

approach the bush. Why does God both attract and yet forbid from drawing near? It is the inevitable effect of holiness upon human beings. When we are first exposed to it, holiness has a beauty which attracts even the most vile sinner. Yet as we enter its presence we are immediately made to understand the cost of intimate contact with God in his holiness. "Take off your sandals, for the place where you are standing is holy ground" (Exodus 3:5). Moses' sandals represent the manner in which he walked in this world. When we walk with our shoes removed we walk very differently than with our shoes on. Thus holiness has this double effect upon us. It first draws us to its beauty yet once we come in contact with it we realize that we can never walk the same again.

That is exactly the effect the church should have in this world. The beauty of holiness in the saints should be attractive to sinners. Yet it should also have the effect of causing the sinner to realize that to remain in fellowship with God's people means to walk differently. Too often sinners are attracted to believers because of the presence of God in them, yet feel no need to change to remain with them.

Inside the Fold's Walls

Besides wrong concepts another reason many believers live in isolation may be found in the normative practice of church life. Modern church life consists for the most part in coming to Christian meetings and has little to do with impacting the world for the Gospel. Most believers are convinced that by supporting church programs they are acceptably serving God. What a pity that being a disciple is no longer determined by one's relationship to the world but by how active one is in church activities. While we certainly believe that true disciples will be involved in the life of the

46

local church that alone should not describe a disciple.

One reason for this has been the manner in which most believers are discipled. After conversion, many believers are encouraged to break all ties with the world. They are told only to watch Christian television, listen to Christian music, read Christian books and have Christian friends. Is it any wonder that soon they are only drinking milk from a Christian cow! Then, after being totally extricated from their former environment they are then told to "win the world for Jesus." So once a week they gather with other believers to pray and engage in a witnessing campaign aimed at reaching total strangers. Commonly called evangelism, this is really more akin to the frenzied eating of a starved shark! Is it any wonder that few ever darken the doors of our churches?

One of our primary needs is to re-examine church structures which encourage believers to live their lives in isolation from unbelievers. Believers must not be allowed to think that serving God means "going to church" and supporting church programs. It is frequently said that it is not so much a matter of church structure as it is a mindset that must be changed. Yet it is naïve to think that there can be a corresponding change

> **D w e l l i n g**
>
> *outside* the
>
> **fold**...
>
> was a **BOON** to the
>
> **CHURCH'S** *ability*
>
> *to* **evangelize**
>
> *the* **world.**

of mindset without a corresponding change of structure. Church leaders may parrot Paul's words that the five-fold ministry is to "equip the saints" (Ephesians 4:11-12), but it will mean little more than sanctified rhetoric if they don't allow people to go outside the walls to do the work. In our day, "equipping the saints" had become the latest buzzword, but the continuance of the status quo has meant that in actuality little has changed.

Outside the Camp

Early Christianity was born outside the walls of the fold. When Jesus said that he had entered the fold to take the sheep out so that they might become the flock, He meant that He was creating a people whose identity would be found totally outside the fold. Their new identity was to be found solely in their relationship to the Shepherd. The early believers took this seriously for no attempts were made to build folds. For three centuries the Christian church existed on this planet apart from many of the things that are now so closely associated with it (church buildings, professional clergy, religious institutions). This is an amazing fact and one that should cause sober reflection. Even more remarkable is that during this same time period, the first three centuries saw the greatest expansion of the kingdom of God of any period in history! Apparently, dwelling outside the fold rather than being a hindrance was a boon to the church's ability to evangelize the world.

One of the reasons for this was the use of believer's homes as the primary meeting place for the young Church. Rather than hiding comfortably in buildings these home meetings provided easy access to those they were trying to reach. They also exhibited the meaning of Christian family which was crucial to the witness of the early church. In such a period of familial disintegration like that of the Post-Augustan Roman Era, God's order for family was powerfully displayed in stark contrast to the norm of the day. All of this meant that the apostolic practice of meeting in homes was a great advantage to the expansion of the Gospel during the Roman Age. We will discuss this more thoroughly in chapter seven.

The *"church as a flock"* allows every believer to live life in full view of the world. All of the exhortations to believers in the New Testament regarding the inevitably of persecution are meaningless unless believers are living their lives in full view of those around them. That is why most believers in the fold are rarely persecuted (unless it is from the brethren). It is only when we leave the fold and enter the flock (like the blind man) that all hell breaks loose! Church life was never intended to be a haven where believers hide out from the world, but a place where they are radically prepared to confront the world with the Gospel. This is no doubt what the writer of Hebrews meant when he exhorted the saints to "go to him outside the camp, bearing the disgrace he bore" (Hebrews 13:13).

CHAPTER FIVE

The Great Shepherd of the Sheep

The first few chapters of this book focused exclusively on Jesus' call to the sheep to leave the fold. The sheep would no longer be characterized as those within the Jewish fold only, but would now be called to leave the fold and be identified with Jesus, the Great Shepherd. This meant the eventual inclusion of the Gentiles who would join their Jewish brethren in becoming "one flock and one shepherd" (John 10:16).

How did Jesus describe the life of his sheep in the flock? Although we have briefly touched on this in this chapter we will seek to provide a fuller picture of how the metaphor of the flock mirrored the new life which the Great Shepherd would give to his people.

When sheep leave the fold it is a most dangerous time for them. Gone is the security of the walls with the shepherd sleeping at the doorway. Once outside the fold's walls there is only one security for the sheep. *It is in their willingness to carefully follow their shepherd and listen to his voice alone.* As the sheep leave the fold their whole identity is found in the relationship they have with the shepherd. For his part he will care for their every need, but for their part they must learn to trust him fully following his lead no matter where he takes them.

In the parable, Jesus made it very clear that he was calling the sheep out of the fold to a new identity with himself. He was the "good shepherd" who was going ahead of them to lead them safely to the rich pasture lands of his life (John 10:3). Their whole identity was now to be found in their relationship to the Shepherd. He is the good Shepherd who demonstrated his care for the sheep by first laying down his own life so that they might be saved (John 10:11,14). In this regard, he is not like one of the "hired hands", but acts only for the welfare of the sheep (10:12-13). These verses are intended to convey to us the care with which Christ Jesus now watches over his flock, attending to each one of the sheep of his pasture.

The Lord is My Shepherd

In the New Testament, Jesus is presented as the "great Shepherd of the sheep" who through his death, resurrection, and ascension secured an abundant salvation for his own (Hebrews 13:20-21). Following Jesus' metaphor of a shepherd and his sheep we are led to think of the great Shepherd-Psalm penned by Israel's shepherd-king, David (Psalm 23). For years, David had been an experienced shepherd in Bethlehem before becoming Israel's glorious king. What better place for the future king of Israel to learn how to lead God's people than by caring for such foolish animals as sheep? David had many deep and impressive spiritual experiences during those years of watching his father's flocks. Many years later he would pen those wonderful words that for all time would best characterize the life of God's people following their great Shepherd-King.

It is helpful to remember that David's great Shepherd-Psalm is actually the middle of a trilogy of Psalms celebrating the salvation history of the Son of God. Psalm 22 is a prophetic revelation of the atoning death of the Lamb of God on Calvary and contains the very words Messiah uttered from his cross; "My God, my God, why have you forsaken me?" (Psalm 22:1, Matthew 27:46). This underscores the basic New Testament teaching that it was the Shepherd's death alone which formed the basis for the people of God. Only by being

> Psalm 23 *portrays* the **Lord's** *present ministry* to *His* people as the **GREAT**
> # Shepherd
> of *His* sheep who leads them through ***ALL of life*** as they **partake** of *His* **FULLNESS.**

the Lamb could Jesus actually become a Shepherd (Revelation 7:17). The Twenty-Third Psalm naturally portrays the Lord's present ministry to his people as the great Shepherd of his sheep who leads them through all of life as they partake of his fullness. Nothing that the sheep will ever need is to be found outside of him who died and rose again on their behalf. The final Psalm in the trilogy (Psalm 24) portrays our Lord's eventual role as King over all the earth. Even though He is already "King of kings and Lord of lords" a day is actually coming when all nations will bow at his feet and acknowledge that fact.

> **NOTHING**
> that the sheep
> will **EVER NEED**
> is to **be found**
> **OUTSIDE** of
> **Him!**

It is the Shepherd's Psalm, of course, that has particular importance in understanding our Lord's teaching in the parable especially regarding the sheep's relationship to himself. The first verse alone is enough to lay a sufficient foundation for Jesus' teaching regarding the most important issue in life in the flock. In the English Bible the first verse reads, "The Lord is my Shepherd; I shall not want." This translation, while straightforward, does not adequately relay the force of the original Hebrew. In the Hebrew text verse one contains only four words — Lord, Shepherd, no want! Could anything be more emphatic? As an experienced shepherd David was responsible for every need of his sheep. When the bear or the lion sought to snatch one of them he personally slew them with his own hands. Years later, reflecting on his relationship with God, David extended that experience to his own relationship to God. He realized that there was nothing in his life that lay outside the purview of Jehovah's care. God was now responsible for every need of his servant. Whenever he found himself therefore in the midst of difficulty and was tempted to doubt

> **Lord,**
> **Shepherd,**
> **NO WANT!**

Jehovah's care he simply remembered the words, "Lord, Shepherd; no want" and was sustained.

That is why this middle Psalm best portrays how the Great Shepherd sustains his people in this present dispensation. Because he has already laid down his life and taken it up again (see John 10:17-18). He has earned the right to be the "Shepherd of the sheep". The entire Psalm portrays the privileges of the sheep under the New Covenant as they follow their Shepherd, Jesus. He is who died for them and now leads the sheep to "springs of living water" (Revelation 7:17). Who would not want to follow this One who willingly laid down his life for the sheep?

All of this corresponds with what the New Testament teaches regarding the Person and work of Jesus Christ. The church was not only founded by him it is also sustained by him and thus remains its central focus. In the simplest designation believers are those who follow the Shepherd. The apostle John saw this very thing so clearly in that passage in the Revelation already quoted (7:17). He spoke of "the Lamb at the center of the throne" who is also "their shepherd" and who leads "them to springs of living water". We should take special note of the fact that it is the Lamb at the center of all of the divine activity. The message is simple: if the sheep want to be where the action is, they must keep their eyes fixed on the Shepherd.

The Sheep Hear the Call

A central aspect of the teaching of the parable of the Good Shepherd is that of the sheep's response to the Shepherd's call (John 10:3-5, 14-16). Jesus makes it clear that everyone who is part of his flock hears his voice and follows him. No room is left for those who hear his voice and do not follow. Just as sheep in a fold will not listen to the voice of a stranger, so when the sheep hear the voice of their Shepherd they will respond and will not follow another.

Later, during the Feast of Dedication, Jesus gave further teaching on this vital matter. It came in the form of some difficult statements he had made as to how the sheep become part of his flock (John 10:22-39). The sheep are those whom the Father had given him and therefore have come to faith in Jesus. Those who are not his sheep cannot believe him (10:26). These statements and others like them are a stumbling-block to many who believe that becoming a member of the flock (kingdom) is merely a matter of human will or decision. While there is no doubt that one must respond to the Gospel upon hearing, the New Testament clearly teaches that only the sheep are able to do so. As Jesus stated so clearly: "my sheep listen to my voice" (John 10:27). A careful reading of Jesus' words in this passage indicates that it is the Shepherd who has chosen the sheep, not the sheep the Shepherd.

Even those opposed to this clear teaching of Scripture are aware, if honest, of the truth of it in their own experience. At a certain moment in their own history they heard the Shepherd calling and began to follow. his voice may have come through another believer, or through a sermon, or some other means, but the result of it was it produced faith in the heart (Romans 10:17). Is this not the ordinary meaning

> A careful **READING** of **Jesus'** words indicates it is the **Shepherd** Who has **CHOSEN** the *sheep,* **NOT** the *sheep* the **Shepherd.**

of grace as found in the New Testament? So much of the emphasis today is often placed on the sinner's need to respond to the Gospel. Yet this blurs the meaning of grace by placing the focus entirely on what the sinner must do. According to Jesus, the reason we believe is not something in ourselves, but that we are the "sheep of his pasture" and that he has called us to himself.

Outside the Fold: A Greater Fullness

The apostolic writers of the New Testament sound out the theme that God's people now live this new life in Jesus outside the fold. This means that the new life of the kingdom can never be confined within the perimeters of Judaism or for that matter any other human religion. We now live under a new covenant, far superior than that of the old. One of the favorite metaphors used by the New Testament writers when speaking of the law is to refer to it as a "shadow of the things that were to come" (Colossians 2:17).

With the dawning of the new covenant they could now say that "the reality, however, is found in Christ" (Colossians 2:17). The writer of Hebrews also makes the point that "the law is only a shadow of the good things that are coming – not the realities themselves" (Hebrews 10:1). None of the apostles disdained the old covenant or treated it contemptuously (as many modern believers do); rather, they viewed it as the covenant which God made with Israel to prepare them for reality (that time when Messiah would come and inaugurate a new covenant). This is what Paul meant when he said that "the law was put in charge to lead us to Christ that we might be justified by faith" (Galatians 3:24). It is not that the old covenant failed; it simply was not able to empower man to carry out God's will. The problem was not with the Law, but with human beings whose sinful flesh made it impossible to keep (Romans 8:3).

Leaving the fold and entering the flock means that the sheep now relate to God on the basis of an entirely new covenant: "For what the law was powerless to do in that it was weakened by the sinful nature, God did by sending his own Son in the likeness of sinful man to be a sin offering. And so he condemned sin in sinful man, in order that the righteous requirements of the law might be fully met in us, who do not live according to the sinful nature but according to the Spirit" (Romans 8:3-4). The whole issue revolved around the need for a "better covenant", a better way of approaching God than that which mankind was given under the old covenant (Hebrews 7:22).

All of this corresponds with the statement in the parable that Jesus came that the sheep might "have life and have it to the full" (John 10:10). This may be the most distorted verse in Scripture. Some have used it to promote a "health and wealth Gospel", distorting Christ's words into a promise of material abundance. To such we would remind them of the words of the apostle Paul who said that those who teach such things are "men of corrupt mind, who have been robbed of the truth" (I Timothy 6:5). Yet what does Christ mean when he promises "life to the full"? We must remember that as far as Scripture is concerned the true essence of life is spiritual, not physical or material. This is how we should understand Christ's promise to a life of abundance. Peter said that God has given us "everything we need for life and godliness through our knowledge of him who called us by his own glory and goodness" (II Peter 1:3). While this certainly does not exclude our physical needs its true meaning is to be found in that which constitutes life indeed – the believer's relationship to God. God has made every provision for his sheep to attain to the fullness of life. No matter what the condition of his people may be, there is abundant provision for them to reach their full potential in Christ. "Life to the full" means nothing less than the full development of divine life in the human soul. This is the Father's purpose for all of his children.

Yet alas, so many of the sheep never seem to attain to their inheritance of fullness of life. One of the reasons is that even though they have been born into the flock their actual experience of the Christian life is, for the most part, still largely confined to the fold with its rules and regulations. Multitudes have never even glimpsed the fullness of life available to them outside the fold. They are still governed by the restrictions of religion (do this; don't

> *"Life* to the *full"* means nothing LESS than the *FULL* development of DIVINE LIFE in the *human soul.*

do this) which characterized the old covenant period. They are still living in *shadows* and not the *substance*. The message of the book of Hebrews applies to them with its strong exhortation to "let us go on" from the various stages of elementary religion to the fullness which has come in Jesus Christ.

Life Based on Knowledge

Jesus made it clear in the parable that each of the sheep would possess a personal *knowledge* of the Shepherd: "I am the good shepherd; I know my sheep and my sheep know me — just as the Father knows me and I know the Father — and I lay down my life for the sheep" (John 10:14-15). In other places in John's Gospel Jesus spoke of that intimate knowledge between himself and his sheep. Even eternal life was more than life without end, but knowing both God and Jesus Christ (17:3). While eternal life certainly implies a quantity of life, Jesus chose rather to emphasize the *quality* of eternal life rather than its *quantity*.

This corresponds perfectly with the Shepherd/sheep motif as presented in the parable. Every shepherd had intimate knowledge of each sheep in the flock and was responsible to care for their every need. They in turn grew in knowledge of him as they learned to trust him for their every need. Is this not intended to instruct us as to the normal course of development in our Christian experience? In his foreknowledge he has known us intimately (I Peter 1:2), yet he has saved us and brought us into a relationship in which our knowledge of him should ever increase until the Day when we will know him even as we are known (I Corinthians 13:12).

The simplest definition of the abundant life promised by Jesus therefore is that it is life in which our knowledge of the great Shepherd is ever growing. God has purposed that each of his sheep grow in the "grace and the knowledge of our Savior Lord Jesus Christ" (II Peter 3:18). Such knowledge is indispensable to the Christian life. It was this that governed the life of the apostle Paul. Near the end of his life and ministry we see him still uttering that great cry which summed up the basis of his whole existence, "that I may know him" (Philippians 3:10). Knowledge of Christ to Paul was everything. The great focus in that life was not the ministry or service for Christ, but the great privilege of knowing Christ Jesus personally. May it ever be so with us.

CHAPTER SIX

The Chief Shepherd

We have already seen that once the sheep leave the fold and enter the flock they have an entirely new relationship with the shepherd. Out of the fold their safety and well-being depend entirely on their willingness to closely follow the shepherd wherever he leads. Gone are the secure walls of the fold protecting them from harm. Now the flock's only security is in their relationship with the shepherd whom they follow. Yet how much better is life outside the fold roaming freely upon the pasture lands and eating to their heart's content.

Jesus intended this flock metaphor to be a fitting type of that life which his sheep would enjoy under the New Covenant. In the previous chapter we saw the implications of that life especially as viewed from the Shepherd/sheep relationship. The Shepherd had willingly laid down his life for the sheep so that "they might have life, and have it to the full" (John 10:10). Each of his own would come to know him intimately and learn to follow him. The great Shepherd-Psalm of David (Psalm Twenty Three) provides the believer with tremendous insights into the fullness of life which our Great Shepherd has ordained for each of the "sheep of his pasture".

> Now the *flock's* **only** *security* is in their **relationship** with the **shepherd** whom they *follow.*

In this chapter we want to see the implications of the flock motif for church life – the unique way that the sheep relate to one another under the rule of the divine Shepherd. The New Testament writers viewed the church essentially as a flock of sheep under the Shepherd's care. We will carefully examine some of the implications of that for the life of the church.

Obviously, the relationship the sheep enjoy with each other differs greatly when they are in the flock than in the fold. All that matters in the fold is that they are protected by the four walls and the sight of the shepherd sleeping at the door. Once they leave the fold their relationship with one another changes drastically. While they must each individually follow the shepherd and listen to his voice, they must also learn how to relate to one another as well. Outside the fold it is relationship with the shepherd and with one another that really counts.

The Flock and the Kingdom

During the earthly ministry of Jesus, he often referred to his followers as a *flock*, drawing on the rich Old Testament portrait of Messiah as a Shepherd and his people the "sheep of his pasture" (Psalm 100:3, Ezekiel 34). In Luke's Gospel Jesus spoke of the flock in the context of his teaching on the kingdom of God (Luke 12:31-32). After exhorting his disciples to seek the kingdom diligently and trusting God for their needs, he reminded them that as his "little flock" he would gladly give them the kingdom. This close connection between the kingdom and the flock meant that his disciples had recognized him as the true Shepherd of Israel and were now seeking to live under his rule, which is essentially what constitutes the kingdom of God.

This teaching of Jesus regarding the flock and the kingdom should remind us of a similar period in the history of his ancient ancestor, David. Before David was officially recognized as king of Israel he spent many years as an outlaw running from his predecessor Saul who sought to kill him. Yet before David ascended to the throne there was a group of men who already decided that David was king and lived as if it was so. These four hundred men came to him while he was hiding in the cave of Adullam and he became captain over them (I Samuel 22:1-2). They had suffered much in Saul's kingdom and now sought relief by joining themselves to David. Living for that time when David would be anointed as God's king, they pledged themselves to remain with him until the day of his coronation. This was the beginning of David's kingdom, this reign over a group of misfits who had first pledged themselves their allegiance to him.

Can you imagine how David and this band of misfits must

have looked; how insignificant this little group must have seemed to the might of Saul's army? Yet David could have easily turned to them and said, "Do not be afraid, little flock, for your Father has been pleased to give you the kingdom." David knew that the day was coming when he would be God's anointed king and they would be with him in the kingdom. In this regard, David perfectly mirrored that relationship between the Lord Jesus and that little flock which was with him. Those disciples had come to him for the same reason that David's men had come to him at the cave of Adullam – they were distressed, in debt, and discontented having lived for so long under that Saulish religious system. Yet it was not only to escape affliction that they had come. They knew that he was the true King of Israel and pledged themselves to faithfully serve him until the Day of his Coronation. And Jesus now assures them that the Father had gladly given them the kingdom (Luke 12:31-32). Just as David's men saw the day of his coronation, even so they would live to see that time when the King of Israel would be coronated through his resurrection and ascension to the right hand of God.

Thus, during his earthly ministry, Jesus commits the kingdom to a small band of faithful men because they knew who he was. They were that *"little flock"* to whom the Lord would commit all of his riches. Yet surely this *"little flock"* paradigm was meant only for the period of his early ministry? As we shall see, even after he accomplished eternal redemption he would continue to identify his followers as that "little flock" to whom he would commit the kingdom.

The Church Under the Chief Shepherd

After his resurrection, the Lord Jesus Christ revealed his purpose for the church in the apostolic writings of the New Testament.

> The *reference* to the **local church** as a *flock* had *more* to do with the **NATURE** of the CHURCH than to its *size*.

In those writings the apostles continue to employ the Shepherd/sheep motif when referring to the church. Numerous passages refer to both Jesus as Shepherd (Matthew 2:6, 9:36, 25:32, 26:31, Mark 14:27, Hebrews 13:20, I Peter 2:25, 5:4), as well as to the local church as a flock (Acts 20:28). Does this indicate that the number of believers in the churches of the Roman world was relatively small? Not at all, though undoubtedly in some places that was true. *The reference to the local church as a flock seemed to have more to do with the nature of the church than to its size.* In other words, even if there were thousands of believers in a city the church functioned as a flock rather than as a fold. This has so many implications, but they can basically be reduced to three: government, function, and leadership. We will deal with government in the rest of this chapter and give each of the others a separate chapter to follow.

We have already seen how the early church viewed the Lord Jesus as the "great Shepherd of the sheep" (Hebrews 13:20). This designation meant more than that he merely cared for the flock. It also meant that the Lord Jesus had the supreme place of honor and authority in the midst of the sheep. This is not immediately apparent to us in the West, but in the world of the Bible there was a close connection between shepherd and ruler (II Samuel 5:2). Many of the ancient kings of Egypt were known as the "Shepherd-Kings". So when the New Testament writers referred to Jesus as the "Chief Shepherd" they meant that he was no mere figurehead, but exercised actual rule over the people of God (I Peter 5:4). He is chief even though there are many shepherds. Jesus holds the

> *The **L o r d Jesus** had the SUPREME place of **honor** and **authority** in the midst of the **sheep**.*

place of supreme authority as the one who leads, directs and cares for the flock.

What did this mean for the actual life of the local church? Everything! No man, regardless of his importance (even Peter who simply calls himself a "fellow-elder") could obscure the vision of the Chief Shepherd as the sole ruler of the people of God. It was not men or their ministries that filled the vision of the apostolic writers but the ascended Lord of glory. They did not merely talk about Christ's position of ascendancy; it was a fact and they lived like it was so. They firmly believed that Jesus was the Shepherd who was fully responsible for all the needs of the flock.

One of the clearest evidences of this is the attitude the New Testament reflects when referring to human leaders. One of the most amazing things is that the majority of New Testament letters were not even written to church leaders at all, but rather to "all the saints" (the exception is the pastoral letters which were not really written to local church leaders but to apostolic co-workers of the apostle Paul). Even in the Corinthian letters where Paul is addressing some of the most serious problems facing any church there is almost no mention of local church leaders. This is not to say that the Early Church was leaderless and that church leaders were unimportant. Indeed in the same context where the writer of Hebrews presents the Lord Jesus as the "great Shepherd of the sheep" he also exhorts them to "obey their leaders and submit to their authority" (Hebrews 13:7). It simply means that church leaders, though present, never obscured the vision of the Lord Jesus in the midst of the flock. The Early Church knew in truth the prophecy of Isaiah that "the government will be on his shoulders" (Isaiah 9:6).

There is much teaching today about proper church government in the church. Yet how many churches are complete strangers to that type of government which is central to God's purpose – the absolute rule of Christ in the church? While most church creeds and doctrinal statements clearly state that the "government is upon his shoulders", in actuality it is not the case. They may recite the creed and sing, "all hail the power of Jesus' name", but then the real authorities take over! The fact remains that in the church today human government has often obscured the divine. Yet it was not always so. Even a scant reading of the book of Acts will reveal that those first believers knew the headship of Jesus Christ in truth. The opening words of Luke's account alone are testimony to that fact. When referring to his previous account (Luke's Gospel), he reminds his readers that it contains "all that Jesus began to do and teach" (Acts 1:1). Apparently, what he now writes is the continuation of Jesus' actions and words through his new body, the Church. For these first believers this is essentially how they viewed the life of the church.

The letters of the New Testament also reveal the practical nature of the headship of Jesus Christ in church life. We would have no letters in the New Testament at all if it was not for the fact that many of the early churches had departed from this vital reality. Some had accepted teaching which relegated Christ to a secondary role, replacing him with angels or some other thing. Others held tenaciously to the creed, yet denied Christ through a lifestyle inconsistent with their confession. Either way it amounted to the same; a denial of Christ's absolute headship in the church. Like Israel of old who rejected Jehovah from being king (I Samuel 8), these churches rejected him who was appointed as "head over all things to the church", replacing him with some form of human substitute. The result was the inevitable loss of divine life. It is always so when Christ is relegated to a secondary role.

CHAPTER SEVEN

The Sheep of His Pasture

I n the previous chapter the truth was underscored that the flock must live under the government of the Chief Shepherd. Though there are certainly under-shepherds which Jesus has given to his church for the care of the flock (we will deal with that in the next chapter), for the sheep there is only One they must follow. The first thing that every sheep must learn to say is, "The Lord is my Shepherd." They must learn to entrust themselves entirely into his hands.

Living under his rule the sheep grow not only in relationship to him, but also with the other sheep in the flock as well. *Church life is the direct result of the sheep's willingness to follow the Shepherd.* In this chapter we will look at some aspects of life in the flock (church life) as the sheep learn to relate to other members of the flock.

> ----•Gↄↄ•----
>
> **Church life** is
>
> the **DIRECT result**
>
> of the *sheep's*
>
> *willingness*
>
> to *follow*
>
> the **Shepherd.**
>
> ----•Cↄↄ•----

It goes without saying that sheep *in the flock* have an entirely different relationship with the sheep than when they are i*n the fold*. The reason for that is the lack of movement in the fold — simply stated, there is none! While they certainly remain safe within the walls of the fold, movement is an impossibility. Besides, there are usually too many sheep within the walls of the fold, and if they move about they will no doubt butt up against the other sheep. No, sheep in a fold have only one real choice and that is to lie down and do nothing! They are not able to eat while they remain in the fold nor can they leave on their own, so there is little more they can do than lie down and wait for that time when they are led out by the shepherd into the green pastures.

What does this have to do with their relationship to the other sheep? In the fold, the other sheep are really unimportant but in the flock each of the sheep must learn to follow the shepherd *as part of the flock*. In other words while their main task is to listen closely to the shepherd, they must also learn to follow as part of a group who follow. How does this relate to true church life as characterized by the flock? It underscores the vital necessity of healthy, accountable relationships in the local church. *In the flock, one must learn to*

> ----•Gↄↄ•----
>
> *Sheep*
>
> must *learn*
>
> to *follow*
>
> the **Shepherd**
>
> as *part*
>
> of the *flock.*
>
> ----•Cↄↄ•----

follow not only the Chief Shepherd, but also learn to relate to all those who also are following. In this chapter we will look at some of the implications of that for church life.

Sheep Means More Than One

The fact the church is referred to in Scripture as a *flock* emphasizes the *corporate nature of the church.* For a flock speaks of several following; isolated sheep never follow a shepherd. The Psalmist reminds us that "we are his people, the sheep of his pasture" (Psalm 100:3). This is a terribly important message for the church today especially in the West. For many Western Christians, faith is essentially an *individual* matter, a personalized affair between themselves and the Lord. If

> For a *flock speaks* of several *following;* isolated sheep NEVER *follow* a **Shepherd.**

they think about the church at all it is only secondarily, a mere afterthought (in some cases not even that). For them the Shepherd has no flock, but only millions of isolated sheep who follow the Shepherd.

It is not entirely improper to lay stress on the believer as an individual for the simple reason that Scripture does. There is an aspect of the believer's life, which is highly personal and private before God. Like that of sheep the metaphor Scripture uses for the believer's personal spiritual life is also drawn from the animal kingdom. It is that of the eagle (Isaiah 40:31). Eagles soar higher than any winged creature and from their high perch are able to detect the smallest rodent moving on the surface of the earth with their radar like vision. *The believer is called to "ride on the heights" (Isaiah 58:14), viewing earthly life from the position of being "seated with Christ in the heavenly places."* And perhaps the most significant thing about the eagle is that the bird is a loner and never travels with others. Have you ever heard of a flock of eagles? In this way, the believer must have a personal spiritual identity apart from others. In the long run each of us rises and falls to God and learns to relate to God for ourselves.

That being said, we are also likened in Scripture to sheep and this is where we speak corporately. This means we must have vital relationship with others in the flock. As one of his sheep I need a relationship not only with the Shepherd, but with all of the sheep among whom I walk the dusty trails. Do you want to know where the Shepherd is? He is to be found only one place – among the sheep of his pasture. The shepherd in the Song told the shepherdess that she must follow the "tracks of the sheep" if she wanted to be with the shepherd (Song of Solomon 1:8).

This is highly antithetical to the individual tenor of much of Christendom today. It is little wonder that many believers become easily bored with the church and even abandon any commitment to her. Since the emphasis is almost entirely on the individual believer many see little need to involve themselves in the life of the church. They reason that if God is only interested in individual believers why bother with the church. Such reasoning, while flawed, is understandable. One can understand how some might thus conclude having spent the entirety of their spiritual lives in an atmosphere where the individual rather than the corporate is highly esteemed.

The alternative is to return to the Biblical emphasis of the church with its corresponding emphasis on "every member". While the New Testament views each individual believer as important the emphasis decidedly lies upon Christ's redemptive work by which He has purchased "a people that are his very own" (Titus 2:14). Peter speaks of them as "a people belonging to God" (I Peter 2:9). Christ's work was not merely to purchase individual believers, but to bring into existence a unique people qualified to serve him. That is what it means to live in the flock. It is to recognize that as an individual believer, I am part of a unique company with whom I now live out this new life in Christ.

Being Built Together

One of the clear differences between life in the fold and life in the flock is that the former requires little or no relationship with the other sheep, while the latter is highly dependent on such relationships. In the fold just being "inside the walls" is what matters – coming to meetings, supporting the programs, etc. In the flock, knowing the other sheep is what really counts. That is why the New Testament presents church life as being primarily a matter of relationships with the Chief Shepherd and one another. And such relationships are not fostered inside church walls. Normal church life in the New Testament is essentially that of a community of believers, each one living out the new life in close proximity with other believers. By community we do not mean a communal lifestyle (although that is certainly an expression of it), but a life lived in close proximity with other believers in the local church.

The New Testament uses three main metaphors to describe the life of God's people; that of a building under construction, a well-ordered family, and finally that of the human body. In likening

> ⸺ ❦ ⸺
>
> *Living stones*
>
> are being **BUILT**
>
> into a **living relationship**
>
> to the **R o c k**
>
> as well as to *other*
>
> *living stones.*
>
> ⸺ ❦ ⸺

believers to a building Jesus and the apostles viewed the church as a building which God himself was erecting, from a metaphor from the world of architecture. Each believer is a separate stone in the structure (Ephesians 2:19-22, I Peter 2:4-5). The idea is that as stones in a building must be solidly together in order to form a structure, so each believer must allow himself to be closely joined to other believers to form the building material of the kingdom. In the passage from First Peter, the apostle Peter may even have in mind the manner by which the Solomonic temple was erected in the Old Testament. The individual stones for the temple were prepared in private so that when they were brought together no tool was needed to dress them (I Kings 6:7). So also, as each believer is prepared in private, he is made to perfectly fit together with those with whom he is being built into the local church.

This also sheds light on the meaning of Jesus' words to Peter that He would "build his church upon the rock" and that the "gates of Hades will not overcome it" (Matthew 16:18). Jesus was preparing Peter and the apostles for that day when they themselves would be involved with him in building the church. *It was essential therefore they understand the nature of that which He was building so cooperation would be possible.* Comparing the passage in First Peter (2:4-5) with Jesus' words to him in Matthew (16:18) it seems that Jesus' preparation of Peter was not in vain. Writing to the church years later, Peter speaks of the Messiah as the "living stone" to whom each one has come closely paralleling Jesus' own words that he would "build his church upon this Rock." *As they have believed upon him each one became a "living stone" and is "being built into a spiritual house" (2:5).* The house of God therefore is comprised entirely of these living stones that are being built into a living relationship to the Rock as well as to other living stones.

For these apostles this was more than theory. When we look at the churches which emerged under their ministries we are not left in the dark as to what they believed about God's house. They erected no buildings but rather built lives into a spiritual house built on one foundation. The genius of apostolic Christianity lies in its simplicity. An apostle would enter a region, preach the Gospel of the kingdom (centered upon the living Stone) with the result that by God's grace some would believe. Those who believed were then formed into a local church comprised of all the believers in that region relating together. Several homes would be used for church meetings with perhaps those occasional times when all the believers would gather together in a larger setting to listen to a visiting apostle. Everything was designed for simplicity and for facilitating relationships. While apostles erected no buildings they certainly left in each locality a building of God —New Testament communities of believers who loved Jesus passionately and who were being built closely together in the bond of love.

All this seems too simplistic for today's complex church world where success is often determined by the number of those gathered and impressive services. Yet the irony is that the same complexities have often meant the loss of vital relationship for God's people. Many who have entered heartily into modern church life have found themselves overwhelmed with Christian activity which, while promising fulfillment, betrays them. *That is because God never ordained for activity to take the place of fellowship.* Certainly we should expect to experience a deepening of relationships as we work together with others. Yet in many churches Christian activity is a substitute for real relationships. Many work side by side for many years yet rarely enter any depth of relationship with those they work with. The notion that participation in church programs and activities is akin to fellowship is erroneous. What is needed is for the living stones in God's house to be vitally built together into a "dwelling in which God lives by his Spirit" (Ephesians 2:22).

> **We see** an ***intense* HUNGER** in **God's** *people* for **real** *relationship* **BOTH** **With** the **Shepherd** and the *sheep.*

There are encouraging signs that God is working today to remedy this dearth of church life even in many traditional churches. The refreshing wind of the Spirit of God is blowing in God's house today and creating thousands of small house gatherings where people are breaking free of the "fold" mentality and experiencing the flock. Unfortunately for many, such meetings are at best a mid-week interval and not the mainstay of church life. And like many other organic New Testament practices the institutional church is assimilating these meetings into its own vortex so that what was originally intended as organic is reduced to technique and programs. Yet, we are encouraged to see the intense hunger in God's people for real relationship both with the Shepherd and the sheep. Surely as this grows there will be a corresponding growth in interest in the apostolic pattern of church life as the means of sustaining vital relationships in God's house.

A Family Affair

The favorite apostolic description of the church in the New Testament is that of the family. Familial terms abound from cover to cover. Believers are referred to as brothers and sisters and apostles are fathers (I Corinthians 4:15). Older women are to be treated as mothers and younger women as sisters (I Timothy 5:2). The central focus of the church gatherings was a "supper", commonly referred to as the "love feast." The church meeting occurred primarily in the homes of the believers. Without doubt, apostolic Christianity produced churches whose members thought of themselves primarily as families rather than institutions. If the church was first and foremost a family its practices must be in keeping with its essential nature.

Today many churches barely resemble a family. Rather, they have taken on more of the appearance of huge corporations instead of simple New Testament assemblies. Pastors of these churches more closely resemble corporate CEO's then Biblical shepherds, running vast and complex institutions dependent on every managerial skill and resource. Occasionally in a small group or cell people may experience a sense of family, but for the most part they are lost in a sea of faces and are easily made to feel like a number or statistic. This is sad especially in light of the fact that our culture has seen a progressive disintegration of the family leaving individuals little opportunity of being nurtured in a normal, familial atmosphere. What an opportunity for the church! Yet so often the church itself has become little more than just another of the complex structures that shield people from a real experience of family rather than promoting it.

That is not to suggest that life in the flock is without appropriate structures. Every healthy family is well ordered with clearly defined lines of authority, discipline, and perimeters. We speak of the "institution of family", and in that sense even the New Testament assembly is an institution (if by institution we mean any pattern of behavior intended to produce a certain affect). Yet a family differs from other institutions in that the members have a unique relationship with each other due to the fact that they have been generated from the same life source. Simply stated, it is life that determines what family I am in.

> There is a **definite,** *discernible* ORDER that *EMERGES* from our *relationship* as a *family*.

Being generated from a common life source and thus members of a family has many implications. For one, informality rather than formality should characterize our times together. It is true that Paul uses the word order to describe New Testament church gatherings, but there is a great difference between familial order and structural organization. In our homes there is a definite order discernible. We take our meals at a certain time, designate family chores, and the children are put to bed at a certain time. Yet it is an order emerging out of our relationship. The main focus is not on the way we do things, but the familial ties and the love we share in the family. So there is a vast difference between the order governing a family and organization governing human institutions. To apply the same hierarchical structures to the kingdom of God used to run IBM is to ignore its essential nature and thus mar its familiar purity.

The New Testament envisions church meetings as having definite order, yet certainly not the highly organized affairs that they have become in modern Christendom (I Corinthians 14). They are meetings of the family and the prevailing atmosphere should be that of informality (yet with order). Family time is fun time (for most families) and church meetings should be highly enjoyable episodes in God's presence and with one another. Those who have grown up in healthy, well balanced families have fond memories of family times. Where else but in the family are we able to "let our hair down" and be real? In the business world or in other societal structures we are often forced to hide our true feelings and deal only on an intellectual or superficial level. Not so when we are at home. There we can relax and let down our guard; after all, our family knows us as we really are anyway.

How far removed this is from the norm in most traditional churches. Rather than openness based on relationship, people tend to hide in large, impersonal gatherings where they remain strangers to others. Is it not sad that most saints are not comfortable to open their lives to others in many churches? Instead of openness and honesty, fear and hiddeness have characterized many churches. This has meant that for many of God's people, there has been little or no experience of family in the local church. *It is sad indeed that many saints are strangers to the body of Christ as family, having spent the entirety of their lives in an atmosphere which more resembles the corporate world than the atmosphere of a well-ordered family.*

Yet there is reason to be hopeful. Many churches are presently encouraging some form of small group as a regular part of local church life. There is an increasing realization that church life must consist of more than merely "going to church" and involvement in programs. Many of God's people are deeply desirous of real relationships in the body of Christ. As this desire has grown so has the willingness to examine long standing church traditions in the light of the apostolic record of the New Testament. This can only lead to an increasing desire among many quarters of the body of Christ to make the plunge "from the fold to the flock".

CHAPTER EIGHT

Life in the Flock

We have already seen that the metaphor of the flock was used by Jesus to introduce the life of the body of Christ under the New Covenant. He was calling the sheep out of the fold (religion) to become the flock. What would life in the flock be like? In the parable, Jesus spoke of it as one of constant movement where the sheep would go "in and go out, and find pasture" (John 10:9). This movement is representative of the free flowing life that would be in the body of Christ, animating and enlivening it so that the sheep would be enabled to follow the Shepherd fully. Without his life the sheep may desire to follow him, but it would be quite impossible. Only as the sheep partake of the life of God can they follow the Shepherd and experience that life of freedom and fullness.

> ⸺ ᏺᏺ ⸺
> **Only**
> as the *sheep*
> **partake** of the
> *life* of **God**
> can they *follow*
> the **Shepherd**
> and *experience* that
> *life* of *freedom*
> and *fullness.*
> ⸺ ᏺᏺ ⸺

It goes without saying that once sheep leave the fold their life is quite unpredictable. Each new day is full of surprises as their shepherd leads them down new paths towards fields of tender green grass. Their job is not to know where they are going, but simply to follow the One who leads. At times they are certainly tempted to think that their shepherd does not know where he is going. Yet he alone knows the way and they must learn to trust him entirely. It is He alone who knows the mountain tracks which, though dangerous, lead to the richest pasture lands.

All of this has its counterpart in church life typified by that of the flock. *Wherever believers exhibit a desire to follow the Shepherd fully, for the most part, there will be both spontaneity and unpredictability.* That is not to suggest that there will be no order and that things are left entirely to the haphazard. Too many of God's people have suffered under the kind of church life that is really not a miracle at all — just the result of poor planning! No, even in the flock, sheep are well ordered as they march forward through the wilderness or over the mountain tracks. Yet it is the shepherd who takes the lead and they merely follow. Like Abraham, the sheep go out "not knowing where they are going" (Hebrews 11:8). So it is that in this sense, real church life was meant to be unpredictable and haphazard.

This is abundantly confirmed in the book of Acts. Luke's

historic account of the early years of the body of Christ testifies to the fact that when affairs are directed by the Lord alone through the Spirit they are quite unpredictable. It has been suggested that Acts should not be entitled "The Acts of the Apostles" but rather, "The Acts of the Risen Lord through his Body, the Church." This is surely a title more in keeping with what we find in that book. As the risen Lord moves out from Jerusalem into the uttermost parts of the earth things are continually changing for the people of God. Think of Peter on the rooftop in Joppa. That man had his entire world turned upside down when the vision came with the command to go and enter the home of a Gentile. We will never know what difficulties that man underwent as he attempted to obey the Lord's word on that occasion. Peter and the other apostles certainly learned that following the risen Lord is not a static thing, something predictable that can be captured and learned by rote. That was what life in the fold had been, but now in the flock they were learning an entirely different manner of life: spontaneously following the risen Lord wherever He goes even when it seems to contradict everything they had previously associated with God's way!

The Flock Gathered

One of the most prolific areas of divine movement is that of church meetings. When rightly understood, the church gathered is one of the most dynamic evidences of the divine nature of the flock. According to Scripture, the gathering together of God's people in the local church is a spontaneous event which tremendously releases God's power. Even unbelievers who come into the midst of a real church meeting may be powerfully persuaded that God is really among his people in truth (I Corinthians 14:24-25).

Our English word "church" is translated from a Greek term

that really means "the called out assembly." It refers specifically to the gathering together of the people of God. Thus the real nature of the church is best seen when her members are gathered together as the church. Even when not gathered they are the church but it is in the act of being gathered that the real nature of the "ecclesia" (Greek word for church) can best be understood. Why? Because the very nature of a church meeting makes manifest the reality of Christ's indwelling each individual

> *The* **Church** *Gathered Is One of the most dynamic* **evidences** OF THE **divine nature** *of the* **flock.**

member of the body. That is because when the church is gathered each member is engaged in that unique work of edifying the members that the redeemed alone can do. *For clearly, the central purpose of the gathering is that the individual members might use their individual gifts to build up the body of Christ* (Ephesians 4:12, I Corinthians 14:26). This is the central reason according to the New Testament knows for our being gathered.

Most of God's people are strangers to this purpose of the church meeting. They know little more than typical meetings in which only relatively few exercise their gifts while the majority sits passively. Indeed, for most it has never even occurred to them that it should be different. They have accepted the idea that only pastors or leaders should speak in the meeting since they alone are qualified to minister to God's people. Thus millions of God's people have spent their lives in an environment in which they have learned only to receive, never exercising that unique gift which Jesus Christ has

given to every member of the body of Christ (I Corinthians 12:7, Ephesians 4:7, I Peter 4:10-11). Is this not one of the major reasons for the gross immaturity and spiritual retardation of the children of God? Like the human body (which the apostle Paul likens the church to), the members of Christ's body also must exercise or else they are weakened. For it is an indisputable principle of spiritual life that only through exercise and use are individual members strengthened and nourished (not to mention the benefit that the members inevitably receive through the exercise of spiritual gifts).

> The **CENTRAL** *purpose*
> of the *gathering*
> IS SO
> *individual*
> **MEMBERS**
> MIGHT USE THEIR
> *individual gifts*
> to **build up**
> the ***body of Christ.***

That this is God's norm for his people will be immediately obvious by a study of four important chapters in Paul's first letter to the Corinthians (I Corinthians 11-14). In those four chapters the whole issue of church meetings is addressed. The Corinthians had apparently written the apostle a previous letter asking him many questions, some of which pertained to church meetings and the exercise of spiritual gifts. Paul begins by addressing their apparent abuse of the Lord's Supper (I Corinthians 11:17-34). Obviously, the apostle sees their coming together to eat the Lord's Supper (which incidentally was an entire meal, not merely bread and a cup) as a normal part of their church meeting (not merely an annual event or a (potluck). Confirmation of that can be found in the book of Acts where Luke records Paul's gathering with the believers at Troas (Acts 20:7). Luke's words clearly point out that on the first day of the week the believers at Troas *gathered*

together to break bread, not merely to listen to Paul preach. It was the Lord's Supper that was the central focus of their gathering – Paul being there and exhorting the disciples was an added blessing. This is a far cry from modern church meetings where the central focus is upon the spoken word while the Lord's Supper is rarely taken and especially not as a meal.

Beginning in chapter twelve of First Corinthians Paul begins answering the various questions the Corinthians had regarding spiritual gifts. He reminds them that though they are one body because of one Spirit (I Corinthians 12:13) they each constituted its various parts (I Corinthians 12:14-31). His whole purpose is remedial; they must learn that the gifts are for the building up of the body not for tearing it down (which they seemed to be doing). This naturally leads to his strong exhortation regarding love. Unless they are ministering out of love, all they are doing is worthless (I Corinthians 13). These two chapters were meant to deal directly with the situation at Corinth in which the saints were using spiritual gifts, not to build one another up, but in a competitive and haughty manner.

In chapter fourteen, Paul deals once again with spiritual gifts, focusing this time on their proper use in assembly meetings. Many of God's people, especially Pentecostal and Charismatic believer have resorted to this chapter to substantiate their beliefs about the importance of spiritual gifts for the church today. This is as it should be since this chapter demonstrates that the exercise of spiritual gifts should be normative in church meetings, something both groups ardently profess. Yet while certain texts are cited (usually the ones referring to tongues and prophecy), what is often completely overlooked is Paul's basic view of a church meeting. This chapter is impossible to understand apart from the apostle's view of a church meeting as that in which every member is engaged in the unique work of *edifying* the body of Christ through the exercise of the *charismas* (gifts). This is not the work of a few gifted ones, nor of the elders only, but that of the entire body of Christ. This does not mean everyone *will* speak in a meeting, but simply everyone *may*.

That this is what Paul taught the Corinthian church should seem incredible to us especially in light of the problems he was seeking to correct in that church. These people were abusing the gifts so that instead of edifying one another they were injuring one another. What would we in the modern church propose as the solution to this problem at Corinth? Being strangers for the most part to that kind of church meeting described here would we not discourage the exercise of the gifts for the more traditional "one man ministry"? Yet that is not what the apostle does. Rather, he exhorts them to continue to

When **God's** *people*

L E A R N

to **bring** the *riches*

of **God's** *grace*

in **Christ**, which

they have been

freely given

then **God's house**

will certainly

be **BUILT.**

exercise spiritual gifts in the church meeting while exhorting them to "try to excel in gifts that build up the church" (12:12). This Paul sees as the normative atmosphere of a church meeting. *When the flock is gathered each member is to be involved in this unique work.*

An Old Testament example will help to underscore this. When God gave Moses the pattern for the Tabernacle he told him to take an offering from the children of Israel, "from each man whose heart prompts him to give" (Exodus 25:2). The Israelites therefore brought the gold and the silver which they had plundered from Egypt and it was out of that material that the Tabernacle was erected. What a wonderful picture this gives of what God expects for New Testament believers. When God's people learn to bring the riches of God's grace in Christ which they have been freely given then God's house will certainly be built. Just as each Israelite contributed to the building of that first house, so today, every believer can bring to a New Testament gathering that unique aspect of Christ's riches which he has been given.

Some may argue there are definitely examples in Scripture in which apostles and other gifted ministers exercised their gifts while the others sat passively and received. That is true and we would be remiss if the impression was given that only meetings where mutual edification occurs are Biblical (which is what some have said). Certainly there is a time and a place for men with gifts of teaching and other gifts to instruct and minister to the flock. It is just that for the most part that is the only type of meeting most saints have known (where the saints sit passively and receive). Too few have known regularly the freedom of which Paul speaks where the church gathers not around a gifted individual, but around the Lord ready to receive what each member brings.

Where the Flock Meets

We have already seen that while folds are relatively large the flock is characteristically smaller. That is why Jesus referred to the small band of disciples during his earthly ministry as a *"little flock"* (Luke 12:32). Yet even after his resurrection when he indwelt his people by his Spirit there was a continuation of this *"little flock"* mentality. Does that mean there were only a small number of believers after his resurrection? We know that was not the case. By the end of the first century the church could be found in every major city of the Roman Empire and that in large numbers. In what sense then did the church continue to be a little flock?

Perhaps one of the reasons for the continuance of the flock mentality was due to the fact that there were no attempts to gather all believers in a locality under one gigantic fold. On the contrary, despite how numerous they were in a given locality the church seemed to be content meeting in the homes of believers. For it is an indisputable fact that for the first three hundred years of church history there is no evidence of any church erecting a building and calling it a church. Was this merely a cultural phenomenon? It was undoubtedly more since both the Jewish and Roman cultures were religiously attached to buildings (synagogues and temples). One would think that the cultural norm would have dictated that the believers meet in buildings rather than houses as the central meeting place.

There are instances in the New Testament of other structures than that of believer's homes being used for meetings (Acts 2:46, 19:6). In the case of the Jerusalem church, Luke is careful to note believers met in both the temple and the homes of other believers. Undoubtedly, the temple meeting was a place for the church to gather to hear apostolic teaching (Acts 2:42). Those who stress church meetings should be held exclusively in homes should be careful not to be legalistic about these matters. The New Testament knows of no fixed pattern that must be followed (although many insist it does). Yet, on the other hand, we must also be careful not to dismiss the centrality of the home as the place where believers gathered so easily. For it is clear from the record of the New Testament homes were the prominent place the Early Church met in the Roman Empire.

Should there be an emphasis on the church meeting in homes today? To answer that we should realize the argument from history alone is inadequate (they did it that way in the First Century so we should do it that way today). The modern church is dealing with scenarios and situations today that the church in Paul's day never dreamed of. It is too easy to say that if the modern church only rid itself of buildings, it would once again discover the life of the New Testament church. Many churches have done just that and have realized their ecclesiastical baggage merely followed them from a building to someone's living room. The more important issue pertains to what was discussed in the previous chapter – the nature of a church meeting itself. *It stands to reason that if church meetings are for mutual edification, affording every member opportunity to exercise his or her gifts for the good of the body, they must be relatively small.* There is some debate from history as to the actual sized of Roman homes, but the best estimate is that they could hold anywhere from thirty of sixty people. In that size of a gathering one can readily understand how each would be free to speak and input into the gathering. Not only would the relative size of the church permit it but also the intimacy enjoyed by the members would insure it. The possibility of mutual edification occurring in a traditional church meeting in a building where hundreds are present is impossible, but when placed in the intimacy of a home with those present who have become vitally joined together is not difficult to imagine.

Taking the three main apostolic metaphors used to describe the church (family, building, body) the home would seem to be the most feasible setting for these to be expressed. If the church is

God's family what better place to express that than in a home with brothers and sisters we have come to know and love? If we are his *building,* the temple where his presence dwells what need is there for an earthly temple? And if we are his *body,* the very members through which he is expressed, what better way to facilitate that than shoulder to shoulder among the other members? In every way, it is the essential nature of the church rather than an argument from history or a cultural expediency that commends the home as the perfect meeting place for the local church.

There is also the argument from experience as well. It cannot be disputed that most churches usually begin in homes: through a Christian worker or perhaps sovereignly, by the wind of the Spirit, several believers are drawn together to meet in a believer's home in a given locality. For a while these meetings are characterized by life and spontaneity. Each week new people are brought to the meetings (even unbelievers) so that one never knows who will come. The meetings themselves while following a general pattern vary from week to week. One week a guitar is strummed and the glory of God descends while the next week a leader spends the entire night teaching the word of God. The meetings can only be characterized as "orderly chaos."

Inevitably, such centers of life will grow numerically and soon that home is no longer suitable to house the meeting. It is at this point a building or other meeting place is sought for the church meeting. As the church moves into this larger facility more and more people are coming and the excitement grows. The former meeting in the home is barely remembered in light of the larger church meeting. Yet quite imperceptibly something else begins to occur. The meetings, once characterized by spontaneity, begin to take on a more *orderly* form. The "orderly disorder" where everyone was free to share and contribute has all but dissipated and in its place has emerged a predictable service where a few participate and the rest sit passively week after week. What has happened? While successful from a numerical standpoint, there is a growing awareness among the members that the church has lost some of its earlier vital elements it once enjoyed (fellowship, accountability, mutual ministry, etc).

What is the recommended solution? *The church must return to meeting in homes if it wishes to regain what it once had.* Without necessarily abandoning its larger meeting[1], it could at this juncture add to it a small group ministry of some sort (cells or home groups) for fellowship, relationship, mutual ministry (real church life). Yet unfortunately, statistics show that the majority of those in the church will never attend these meetings in homes once having come into the church through the large group format.

Is there another option? Once having outgrown that initial home the church could have begun to meet in a second or third home rather than abandon church life in homes altogether. Resisting the temptation to gather all the sheep into a large fold, these flock meetings would have insured the continuance of mutual ministry and spontaneity. Provision could have been made to occasionally gather these house churches together in a larger

---

1. It is interesting to note that in the parable of the Good Shepherd Jesus made mention of the sheep going "in and out", a clear reference to the fold as well as the flock. In this book the emphasis has been decidedly on the sheep leaving the fold, yet here Jesus seems to suggest that their life will consist of going both in and out. Without pressing this too far, perhaps this lends Biblical credence to the fact Jesus envisioned the local church in its various localities to experience both larger (fold) and smaller (flock) gatherings. Certainly, the Corinthian letter suggests that though the church consisted of many different house churches throughout the city, at least at times the church as a whole came together in one place (I Corinthians 11:20, 14:23). Those who lay stress only on the smaller house meetings should consider these things.

setting for ministry when necessary, especially for ministry from a gifted person (Ephesians 4:11) without abandoning the real basis for church life.

There is tremendous pressure on a church that begins in a home to legitimize itself and move up to a larger setting. Many have bought into the idea that real growth can only occur by moving into a building that can accommodate the numbers. A small house church seems hardly able to compete with the large folds that seem to gather people effortlessly. Yet what is lost in the process is rarely considered (intimacy, accountability, relatedness, mutual responsibility). In the desire for quantity there is often an abandonment of quality. Many of the larger churches are presently recognizing the need for these small groups settings to provide an atmosphere for God's people to properly grow.

> *If we* **STRESS** an **OUTWARD** PATTERN **RATHER THAN AN** *inward life* — *we will* INEVITABLY become **narrow.**

The Real Issue

We must not be dogmatic about these things. It is not where the flock meets that is the most important issue. *The real issue is that of being gathered around the Lord alone.* If we stress an outward pattern rather than an inward life we will inevitably become narrow. While we should be concerned with the pattern of things as found in the New Testament the emphasis should always be upon life.

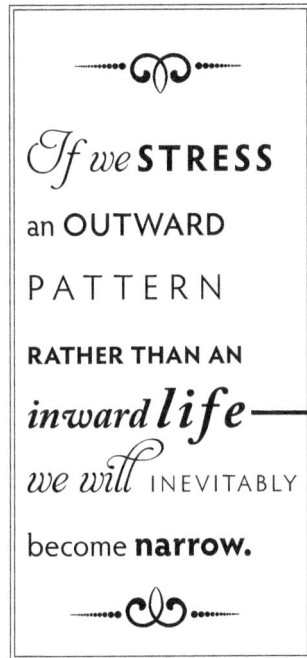

The truth is, there are many churches that have little concern for the pattern yet are depositories of life. There are also others where great emphasis is laid on the "proper pattern of things" while there is an absence of life.

We must realize these are not mutually exclusive. Those who stress life without concern for any discernible pattern would do well to consider what the New Testament says regarding the outward aspects of church life. Yet they should do so not in order to slavishly imitate a pattern, but to understand how to best express the inward life they possess in Christ. On the other hand, those whose emphasis is the *pattern of things* need to be careful not to stress the outward form of things to the exclusion of real life. It is so easy to lay claim to New Testament reality based solely on an outward form that they maintain. We have seen that life in the flock is first a matter of the Shepherd himself directing each of his sheep by his Spirit into relationship with himself and then with the other sheep. It is always first a matter of life. Yet it is life *in the flock* and that implies a certain form (although not rigidly). We should expect that wherever people are caught up in a flow of life there will be certain distinguishing marks regarding their church life.

www.ingramcontent.com/pod-product-compliance
Lightning Source LLC
Chambersburg PA
CBHW071623040426
42452CB00009B/1453